Dummies and pacifiers

Dummies and pacifiers can also be very damaging to language development, particularly when they are used all day. This use restricts the development of speech by reducing the muscular development within the mouth and tongue, as well as endangering the formation of teeth. Practitioners will need to handle this information sensitively when talking to parents, and encourage them to restrict the use of dummies and pacifiers to sleep time or when the child is distressed. Children who crawl, walk or run around with a dummy or feeding cup constantly in their mouth endanger their language development and may endanger their personal safety if they fall. Settings should consider whether to include guidance on dummies, pacifiers and feeding cups in their policies and procedures as well as in their prospectus or guidance to parents.

The role of the Key Person in communication

The role of key person is vital to the success of 'Sounds Fun' activities. Close bonding between key adults and the babies and children in your setting will create a firm foundation for language development. Key members of staff know each child and their family well, and they are in a unique position to nurture language and social development. Their observations will be vital in deciding which activities to plan for the child, and they can create the warm, welcoming and informed link with the child's family.

The key child or key group is at the heart of these activities. They are ideal for key group times, so build them into your daily programme, using individual and small group times for talking, listening, singing and rhymes. Create comfortable places indoors and outside for these key times – settees, armchairs, swing seats, garden benches, bean bags, cushions and rugs are all useful places for language activities where babies and children feel at ease.

Remember that the language you use is crucial to babies' and children's own language development. Use appropriate language whenever you are with children, even if you think they can't hear or are not listening. Children are like sponges and they will soak up your language, whoever you are talking to, and whatever they appear to be doing at the time.

Some tips are:

- If you use 'baby language' such as 'baa-lamb', 'moo-cow' or 'quack-quack' you will restrict children's language development. As a professional you need to help children to learn and use the proper names for animals and objects.
- Don't use slang or 'street language', and discourage others in your setting from using it too. You may need to discuss this as a group and even decide which words are unsuitable. We sometimes use unsuitable words without thinking, and are surprised when children repeat them back to us, or use them in their play.
- Local words or dialect words are part of children's world, but you do need to help them
  to use a range of words, including alternatives to the local ones.

Introduction

Children with additional needs

As Key person you have a responsibility to identify, and if necessary seek help for, children with additional needs. Your setting will have a policy for the support of these children, and if you observe extreme difficulties you should follow the procedures in the policy.

However, some babies and children have developmental delays, which are less severe and can be supported by adapting the activities to make them simpler or less demanding. Other options include choosing activities from an earlier book, or limiting the length of time or the size of the group for the activities you choose. Observation, note-taking and consultation with colleagues and parents will help you to get the right match of activity for each child.

Taking the activities outside

Some children love being outside, are naturally more focused there, and learn best in an outdoor environment, where the sounds, sights, colours and smells are so different from indoors. Outdoor play is now a requirement within the Early Years Foundation Stage, and we have supported this requirement by embedding outdoor activities in all four Sounds Fun books. Each activity in each book has suggestions for taking the idea out of doors, regardless of whether you have a large or small outdoor area.

Some settings have ideal outdoor spaces but of course some of you are providing outdoor experiences in gardens, parks, playgrounds, community spaces or even the balcony of your flat! These are all suitable places for taking 'Talking Time' out of doors and we hope you will adapt the suggestions to fit your own circumstances.

Of course, every setting has its own policies and procedures for outdoor play, and we would strongly advise that you continue to follow these, as every setting is different. However, we would like to add some specific guidance for the 'Talking Time' activities, which we hope will help you to make the most of your outdoor area.

Your outdoor area should include spaces for stillness and quiet reflection, away from the busy bikes and ball play. These places could include seats and benches, grassy areas, pop-up tents and other shelters, blankets, mats, cushions, sleeping bags, groundsheets or mattresses. Use these areas for individual or small group times for talking, listening, story telling or singing, and be there in all weathers and during all four seasons. A Place to Talk Outside by Elizabeth Jarman (Featherstone) has some excellent ideas for making sure outdoor spaces are the kind of places young children will develop their language skills.

Involving parents

These books contain a wealth of suggestions for working with parents, and simple ideas for activities parents will be able to do to support their children's learning. The section 'Involving parents' included with each activity suggests things that parents can do at home, things they can bring to show at the setting and other ideas for simple home-based resources.

How will 'Sounds Fun' activities help you?

This series of books is intended to help you help children with sounds, words, talking and reading.

The activities:

- expand the work you are already doing in your own setting to ensure that every child becomes a confident talker and listener – with the best foundations for later speaking, listening, reading and writing;
- supp ort your work with individual children and groups within the Key person process;
- help you in your work with parents, who are children's first and most influential educators;
- provide stimulating and varied activities, carefully matched to the developmental stages in your setting, from babies to children of Reception age, where the activities will be useful support for your phonics sessions.

Which age range are the activities suitable for?

Every activity is presented in the same format to make it easier for you to use within your own planning framework. For ease of use, we have divided the activities into four age ranges, covering the whole of the Early Years Foundation Stage:

- Book 1 covers developmental stages 1 and 2: babies from birth to 20 months (Babies)
- Book 2 covers developmental stages 3 and 4: babies and children from 16 to 36 months (Toddlers)
- Book 3 focuses on development stage 5: children from 30-50 months (Pre-school)
- Book 4 focuses on development stage 6: children from 40 – 60+ months (Reception)

Of course, if you have children whose communication levels are high, you may want to dip into the next book in the series, and if you have children who have individual needs or would benefit from more reinforcement at an earlier stage, you can refer to earlier books.

What's inside each book?

Each book contains 35 activities, each on a double page spread and featuring:

- The focus activity (What you need, what you do and what you say);
- How you could **enhance** the activity by adding more or different resources;
- How you can **extend** the activity for older children or different sized groups;
- Taking the activity **outside** into your garden, a park or other play area;
- Suggestions for **songs, rhymes and stories**;
- **Key vocabulary and gestures** for you to use during the activity;
- Suggestions for **things to look for** as you observe the children during the activity (Look, listen and note);
- How to **use the activity with parents**, either by adapting for home use, or involving parents in your work in the setting.

Some activities will become favourites with the babies and children, and you will return to them again and again in your daily routine, building them into such times as snack, changing and rest times, as well as in the introduction to stories and song sessions.

In the bag

This core activity is suitable for a small group of children.

What you need:

A fabric bag with a drawstring (make one from an old pillowcase)

A few familiar objects such as a sock, a Lego brick, a toy car, a puppet, a pair of boots and a camera

A small cloth, such as a tea towel.

Involving parents

You could...
- *Have the activity out and show the parents how to do it.*
- *Take photos and display them so parents can see how you do the activity.*
- *Talk to parents about using objects from their home for this activity.*
- *Display some suitable everyday objects to use for this game, and some suggestions for simple bags or other hiding places.*

All children love guessing games, and this is an extension of 'In the box' from *Sounds Fun 16 - 36 months*. The use of familiar objects and a simple cloth bag will encourage early language, thinking and describing. Play it anywhere with any object that will ft in your bag

What you do

1 Show the bag to the children and explain that you are going to play a game together. Show them the objects you have collected (not more than four to start with), naming each one and then passing it round the group for the children to feel.
2 Cover all the objects with a cloth.
3 Now, ask the children to cover their eyes as you hide one of the objects in the bag.
4 Give the children a clue to the missing object e.g. 'It's soft and you put it on your foot'.
5 Let the children guess which object is hidden in the bag. If they find it difficult, give them another clue, or take the cover off the other objects and see if they can spot which one is missing.
6 When everyone has had a guess, let one child tip out the object and see if they were right.
7 Play again with another object.

Extending the challenge

- Choose pairs of objects such as a knife and a fork, a cup and a saucer or a sock and a shoe. Put a pair of items in the bag. See if the children can name one of the pair, or even both.
- Give the lead role to a child and let them choose an object to put in the bag and then make up a clue to help the other children guess.
- As children get better at this game, use some very similar objects that need more careful and detailed clues e.g. bricks of different shapes and sizes, books with different titles or a collection of clothes or shoes.

Look, listen and note

- *Look for the children who listen to clues about the object, not just guessing?*
- *Can the children guess what the objects are and then talk about them?*
- *Do they use phrases such as 'I think…'*
- *Do they stay engaged in the game?*

TOP TIP
This activity doesn't need expensive resources – just a bag and a few everyday objects!

Enhancing the activity

- Choose pairs of objects such as a red sock and a blue sock or a police car and a fire engine.
- Collect some objects that link with a current topic.
- Use objects that all start with the same sound e.g. a brick, a boat, a beaker and a ball.
- Read books such as *Who's Hiding on the Farm*, by Fiona Watt (Usborne), *Who's Hiding at Home?* By Julie Fletcher (Campbell Books), *What's Hiding in There?* By Daniela Drescher (Floris Books).

Take it outside

- Have an 'Outside guessing bag' and use some familiar natural objects such as a fir cone, shell, stick, leaves or grass.
- Let the children collect some objects to play the game.
- Bring objects back from walks and visits.

♪ Sing a song about the box – try these words to *Twinkle, twinkle little star*:
Close your eyes and wait to find
What is hiding round behind.
Can you guess, wait for the clue
This will give some help to you.
Close your eyes and wait to find
What is hiding round behind.

Key words and gestures

- Listen (with your hand behind your ear)
- Still (with your hand held up, palm forward)
- Wait
- Guess

- Behind
- Missing
- Turn
- Clue
- Think
- Right

Walks outside

This activity is suitable for any number of children.

What you need:

No special equipment, just an indoor or outdoor space anywhere

Focusing on sounds in the world around is an essential part of developing listening skills. Young children need frequent opportunities for this listening outdoor experience. You don't need to spend long, just pop outside, or stop and listen during walks and other outdoor experiences.

Enhancing the activity

- Take your 'Talking-time puppet' with you to help with focus and fun.
- Hide a ticking timer or hang a bell from a bush.
- Ask the children to point to the source of sounds when they can't see the object.
- Read *The Listening Walk* by Paul Showers (HarperCollins), Noisy Poems by Jill Bennett (OUP), *No One's Listening!* By B. Birney (West Publishing), *The Listening Walk* by David Kirk (Grosset and Dunlap) or *Rosie's Walk* by Pat Hutchins (Bodley Head) – a great book with no words.

What you do

1 Take a walk in your garden, play area or local community.
2 Make sure there are plenty of opportunities to sit and talk. In your garden, make some 'talking corners' where children can sit and chat to each other and to adults. A park bench, low wall or a blanket on the grass would be a good place if you are further afield. You need to be close enough to the children for them to see your face and hear what's going on.
3 Listen together to the sounds you can hear – these may be urban, garden or rural, depending on where you are.
4 Ask the children if they can hear anything, encouraging them to look for the sound and name what or who is making it.
5 Listen carefully yourself, turning your head so you can hear all round, then choose a sound to focus on – a bird, a car, children playing, distant traffic or a fire engine.
6 If you can see the source of the sound, look at it, and use your gaze to help the children focus on it too.
7 Talk about the sounds you can hear e.g. 'I can hear a dog barking. Where do you think it is? Why do you think it's barking?'
8 Don't talk so much that the children can't hear the sounds! Encourage quiet and calm.
9 Take turns with the children in choosing a sound to talk about. Give them plenty of thinking time.
10 Don't go on too long, listening is a concentrated activity – little and often is the best way to improve listening skills.

Extending the challenge

- Listen for smaller sounds such as paper blowing in the wind, leaves rustling or footsteps.
- Take photos of the sounds you have heard outside. Make these into a 'Listening walk' book, adding more photos as you hear new sounds.

Look, listen and note

- *Look for children who still find it difficult to sit and concentrate.*
- *Note the children who are really good at listening and focusing, you may want to give these children the more challenging activities, or let them be the leader.*
- *Keep a careful note of any child who seems to be having difficulty hearing sounds. They may need a hearing test if this doesn't improve.*

Key words and gestures

- Listen
- Look
- Can you hear?
- Show me where
- Sound
- Who/what
- Loud/soft
- Sky
- Ground
- Near/far away

TOP TIP

Remember, some children find it difficult to walk and talk at the same time!

Take it outside

- Go for listening walks in every season. There is just as much to hear in the winter, or on a rainy day. Foggy days are even better for focusing on listening skills.
- Hang some small sound makers such as little bells, shells or old metal cutlery in bushes and trees so children can follow a listening trail.
- Try sitting with your hands over your eyes, or cupped behind your ears, and see if this helps with listening.

Involving parents

You could...
- *Suggest listening walks as a simple activity, even during a shopping trip.*
- *Remind parents that listening is a key to talking, so children need plenty of experience of the human voice and seeing adult faces in conversations.*
- *Encourage parents to get down to their child's level when speaking to them, and make frequent eye contact with their child when they want them to listen.*

Teddy's lost

This activity is suitable for a small group of children.

What you need:

A teddy, doll or soft toy

Ideally, 2 adults

A game based on the traditional one of 'Hunt the thimble' where children use clapping to indicate 'Getting warmer' and 'Getting colder' to help the hunter to find the toy. At first the 'hunter' may need an adult to help them find the hidden toy.

Enhancing the activity

- Use a figure or object linked to a favourite book or TV programme.
- Once they are used to the game, let children be hunters in pairs.
- Hide the object low down or behind something, to make the game more interesting.

♩ Sing this song to the tune of *I hear thunder* before the hunter starts to look for the object:
Teddy's hiding,
Teddy's hiding
Where is he? Where is he?
Am I getting warmer?
Am I getting warmer?
Please help me. Please help me.

What you do

1 Sit in a circle and hold the teddy on your knee.
2 Tell the children that you are going to hide the teddy (or another soft toy) somewhere in the room, and one child can look for him, while the others help by clapping to tell them how near they are to the teddy.
3 Do a practice run by putting the teddy somewhere in the room and asking the other adult to be the 'hunter'.
4 Help the children to understand about clapping softly when the hunter is far away from the toy and louder when they get nearer.
5 Now ask for a volunteer child to play the game again.
6 This child and the second adult must cover their eyes while you or a child put the teddy somewhere in the room. When you first play the game, make sure you put the teddy somewhere fairly obvious!
7 Now the group can begin to clap as the hunter opens their eyes and begins to search for the teddy.
8 When the hunter has found the teddy, play once more.

Key words and gestures

- Listen
- Louder
- Softer
- High
- Low
- Nearer
- Hiding
- Turn

Extending the challenge

- Use something smaller, such as a toy car or a small world figure.
- Ask the hunter and their helper adult to go out of the room. Then ask all the children to close their eyes while you hide the object. Let the group open their eyes and spot the object before the hunter comes back in the room.
- Sing a song while the hunter is looking, singing louder and softer to help them find the object.

Look, listen and note

- Watch to see how engaged the children are when they are not the hunter.
- How well can individual children adapt the volume of clapping to help the hunter?
- Can the children hear the louder/softer clapping?
- How carefully do individual children look and follow the sound clues when they are the hunter?

Take it outside

- Play the game outside using a natural object such as a cone or shell.
- Hide an object before the children come outside and sit where they can hear you clapping the clues.
- Take a teddy or other soft toy with you when you go on walks and outings so you can play the game in different places.

Involving parents

You could...
- *Tell them about the game and suggest they play it as a family – they could try it at the park or on the beach.*
- *Suggest they hide a small snack item, such as an apple or a small biscuit, and help the child to find it by clapping.*

TOP TIP
Practise clapping loudly and softly as you sing or listen to the radio or a CD.

Ears hear

This core activity is suitable for a small group of children.

What you need:

A selection (not more than three) of sound-makers, such as timers or wind-up musical toys.

An improvised screen such as a big open book or an easel to hide the sound makers.

Enhancing the activity

- Add another sound-maker, so you have four.
- Play this game with simple, hand-held musical instruments such as shakers, rattles or bells.
- Play the game in different areas of the setting so children must listen harder to hear the difference.

♪ Sing this song to the tune of *I hear thunder*:
What is hiding? What is hiding?
I can't see, I can't see.
We just have to listen;
we just have to listen,
Carefully, carefully.

This activity extends 'Tick-tock' in *Sounds Fun 30-50 months* by giving children a more complex listening challenge, using the same sound-makers and wind-up toys.

What you do

1. Sit somewhere quiet.
2. Show the children the sound-makers, say the name of each one, and listen to the sound each one makes.
3. Now tell the children you are going to put all the sound-makers behind the screen and just turn one on.
4. Put all three sound-makers behind the screen and turn one on.
5. Let the children listen and guess which one it is.
6. Play again with either the same sound or a different one, until you have used all three.
7. Give plenty of praise for guessing and naming.

Look, listen and note

- *Note the children who can hear the object but not discriminate what it is.*
- *Look for children who struggle to play the game when they can't see the object. These children need more practice in smaller groups or one-to-one.*
- *Be aware of health or seasonal differences in some children's listening skills.*

Involving parents

You could...
- *Suggest parents play this game by hiding a sound-maker inside a cupboard.*
- *Collect some sound-making objects for your loan collection or toy library.*

Key words and gestures

- Wait
- Listen
- Choose
- Which one?
- Tick
- Sound
- Loud/soft

Take it outside

- This game is more difficult to play out of doors, so you will need noisier items, such as a drum, a cymbal or a CD player.
- Hang a sheet or blanket from a line to make a screen for this and other listening games.
- Make an outdoor 'listening corner' in a quiet part of your garden.

Extending the challenge

- Choose some similar sound-makers, maybe two timers that have different 'ticks'.
- Let the children take turns to sit behind the screen and choose a sound-maker to turn on.
- Collect some sound-makers that make softer sounds.

TOP TIP
Use an old mobile phone and alter the ring tones.

I went to the shops

This core activity is suitable for a small group of children.

What you need:

A shopping basket (big enough to see what's inside)

Some familiar items such as a bag of crisps, a packet of biscuits, an apple, an egg box, a packet of cereal, a juice box and a yogurt. Real objects are better than plastic replicas for children of this age.

Involving parents

You could...
- Suggest that this is a good game to play in the car or on the bus. They may remember it from their childhood.
- Encourage parents to help their children remember objects in order, by talking about what has happened during the day, starting with getting up.
- Have some simple sequencing games for parents to borrow and play at home. Take photos of simple activities such as putting on socks and shoes, getting dressed, making dough or mixing paint and painting a picture.

This version of an old game challenges children to remember items in sequence, with the added support of the objects they are recalling. Watch carefully to make sure that the number of objects to remember is manageable.

What you do

1 Sit together in a circle and talk about the game you are going to play.
2 Look at and name each of the items, passing them round the circle.
3 Put all the items and the basket in the middle of the circle.
4 Start the game yourself to show them how to play. Say 'I went to the shop and I bought... an apple.' Choose the apple, name it and put it in the basket.
5 Pass the basket to one of the children and help them to say 'I went to the shop and I bought...' They must say the name of your chosen item before choosing an item of their own and naming that e.g. 'I went to the shop and I bought an apple and a packet of crisps.'
6 Continue to play, as children add an item of their choice to the end of the list. Encourage them to really listen and name the objects in order.
7 When everyone has had a turn, take all the items out of the basket and ask the group if they would like to play again.

Key words and gestures

- Basket
- Remember
- Turn
- Listen
- Order
- Choose
- Watch
- List
- First, second, next, last

Extending the challenge

- As children get better at this game, they can play in a bigger group, with more items to remember.
- Make some laminated cards by taking photos of familiar i tems and using these instead of actual objects.
- Read Don't Forget the Bacon by Pat Hutchins (Red Fox) or The Shopping Basket by John Burningham (Red Fox).

Look, listen and note

- *Look carefully to make sure the children can cope with the group size. Some children may need to practise this game in very small groups.*
- *As you make the game more difficult, note those children who find it hard to remember things in order. Help them to listen and look carefully.*
- *Some children will become very good at this game. Challenge these children by playing the game without the objects.*

Take it outside

- Play this game outside on a blanket under a tree or other shelter. You could have a shop out of doors and really go shopping in the game.
- Play 'I went to the garden centre or the garage'. Or play 'I went to the park and I found...'
- Play the game when you are on a walk or visit or go shopping for real and choose one thing each, then play the game when you get back to your setting.

Enhancing the activity

- Try the same game with just fruit, vegetables, pet foods, clothes or toys and play 'I went to the... greengrocers, the pet shop, the toy shop, the clothes shop.
- Play with small world animals or toy cars and go to the zoo or the car showroom.
- Leave the game in the book corner or the role-play area so children can play it independently.

♪ Sing this song to the tune of *Here we go round the Mulberry bush* remembering what each child bought:
*We will play the shopping game, the shopping game, the shopping game,
We will play the shopping game. Can you remember well?
(Child's name) bought a cereal bar, a cereal bar, a cereal bar,
(Child's name) bought a cereal bar, who went shopping next?*

TOP TIP
Make sure you have some child-sized baskets and bags for informal shopping experiences.

Echo me

This core activity is suitable for a small group of children.

Copying an adult's voice and actions is a simple game that can be used at any time by any adult with any child in the group. This can be a small group or 'anytime' game to encourage concentration and imitation.

What you do

1 Sit with the children and say 'We're going to play Echo Me'. Do you know how to play? I say something or do something and you copy me.'
2 Practise by saying simple single words such as 'Hello' or 'Good morning'.
3 If you have a 'Talking-time puppet', use it to help the children to focus.
4 Now try some of these:
5 Two claps of your hands
6 Click your fingers
7 'Pop' your cheeks
8 Slap your knees
9 Make some mouth music such as 'lalala' 'mmmm'
10 Say some simple words, such as 'click and clap', as you do the movements.

Take it outside

- Play a more physical version out of doors, jumping, clapping, stamping or hopping.
- Teach the children how to play 'Simon says'.
- Have a 'Follow my leader' parade round the play area, making sounds and movements.

Involving parents

You could...
- *Take a short video of the children playing this game to show parents what good fun it can be. This may encourage them to play it with their children at home.*
- *Find some simple board books that encourage movement rhymes and games such as Heads Shoulders Knees and Toes; The Wheels on the Bus; If You're Happy; Incy Wincey Spider; Twinkle, Twinkle; Row your Boat by Annie Kluber (Child's Play)*

Look, listen and note

- *Watch for children who need much simpler movements or sounds to copy, and work one-to-one with these children.*
- *Note the children who find this game easy and fun. Use them as leaders sometimes.*
- *Look at the way children copy your movements and sounds, and use this game as an opportunity to practise movements that the children find more difficult.*

Extending the challenge

- Make a short series of sounds or movements (not more than three), such as clap, clap, slap, make a face AND pull your ears, clap AND stamp.
- Pass the sound or movement round the group from child to child.
- Let the children make a sound and movement combination for the group to echo.

Enhancing the activity

- Give each child a paper or plastic plate and a chopstick to copy tapping sounds and patterns.
- Let each child sit with a teddy or soft toy in front of them, holding the toy's arms and making them do the echo. Some children find this much more engaging.
- Let a child be the leader for you all to echo.

♪ Sing:
*Let everybody clap hands, clap hands, clap hands,
Let everybody clap hands, just like me.
(Let everybody stand up; sit down; march round; make a face; clean your teeth etc.)*

- Read *Little Beaver and the Echo* by Amy MacDonald (Walker Books)

Key words and gestures

- Look
- Listen
- Copy
- Follow
- Leader
- Echo
- Watch

TOP TIP
Use this game at different times of the day when you have a spare minute.

Tell me where

This core activity is suitable for a small group of children

What you need:

A collection of small world toys from a farm, a zoo or a town etc

A play mat, tray or other environment for the game

Involving parents

You could...
- *Talk to parents about simple 'hide and find' games and how they can hide something then give their children clues to find it.*
- *Use books, magazine pictures and other visual materials to play spotting games.*

Playing with familiar objects and toys, such as small world, is a good way to begin to explore positional language as well as encouraging children to look carefully.

What you do

1   Spend time with the children, setting out the farm, zoo, park, airport, roadway or whatever you have. Talk about the animals, people, vehicles and equipment as you work, making sure the children know the names of all the people, animals and other pieces.
2   When you have set out the scene and let the children explore it, suggest a game called 'Tell me where'.
3   Start to ask the children questions about the objects: *'Where's the elephant?' 'Can you see something red?' 'Who's next to the slide?' 'Where's the baby in the pram?'* Encourage the children to say the answers, not just point, and praise them when they do. Repeat their answers back to reinforce words and phrases e.g. *'Yes, the baby is by the swings.'*

Take it outside

- Draw a roadway in chalk on the path or patio for a new game with cars or other vehicles.
- Use boxes and other construction equipment to explore position and observation.
- Play 'hide and seek' with objects as well as people and give clues to find them.

Key words and gestures

- Play
- Look
- Carefully
- Behind
- In front

- Under
- Between
- Next to
- Near
- Inside

TOP TIP
Wrapping paper is a good source of complex pictures and patterns.

Look, listen and note

- *Note children who don't appear to be able to differentiate between position words and give them more help and support in learning about the positions of things.*
- *Watch for children who really enjoy this sort of observational game and make it more challenging by adding instructions or offering some treasure hunt books or simple computer games.*

Enhancing the activity

- Use a scene like this to work on positional words. Ask children to put named objects in, on top, behind, under, next to etc.
- Use empty cardboard boxes or cartons and soft toys to play similar games of location and position.
- All these games can be enhanced by asking the children to put objects, small world toys or soft toys in, on, under, behind or in front of different parts of the scene.

Extending the challenge

- Play whole body position games in your room. Ask children to put themselves in, on, under, behind etc. using pieces of furniture, fabrics, and other objects in your environment.
- Give two instructions or two pieces of information, such as: 'Can you point to a dog and a baby?' 'Where is the black and white cow?'
- Play a game where children must follow your instructions with positional vocabulary e.g. 'Put your finger on your nose and your other hand under your leg.'

♩ Sing: *Put your finger in the air, Heads, shoulders, knees and toes, or One finger, one thumb keep moving.* 'Read: *Head, Shoulders, Knees and Toes: Clap, Wriggle, Stretch and Jump* by Brian Moses (Franklin Watts) *Toddler Play* by Dr Wendy S Masi (Creative Publishing International) *Okki-Tokki-Unga: Action Songs* for Children by Beatrice Harrop (A & C Black) *Where's Wally?* by Martin Handford (Walker Books)

Mystery sounds

This core activity is suitable for group or class of children.

Your 'Talking - Time' puppet or a soft toy (a puppet or soft toy that is only used during 'Talking - Time' sessions)

A number of sound-makers such as a toy phone, a kitchen timer, some pebbles in a tin, a wind - up toy with a noisy key, a small musical box, an alarm clock with a loud tick, a rattle or a shaker

A washing line with some fabric pegged on it or a large book or something else to make a screen in front of the objects.

Involving parents

You could...
- *Share the game with parents, by lending cards and recorders to use at home.*
- *Recording sounds on a mobile phone is a really easy way to play this game.*
- *Explain how to play 'I hear with my little ear'.*

Making sounds for children to recognise is one really good way of playing with sounds. This simple activity with objects can easily be extended by using a tape recorder or Dictaphone. It is also another opportunity to use a 'Talking-time puppet'.

What you do

1. Remind the children of the name and the purpose of the 'Talking - Time' puppet.
2. Now look together at the sound-makers you have collected. Make sure the children can name them all and hear the sounds they make.
3. Now put your screen up or draw the fabric in front of the objects, so it covers the 'Talking - Time' puppet (or your hand and arm).
4. Name one child and say: 'Listen to the sound. Can you say what it is?'
5. Make the sound behind the screen, and let the child guess which object made it.
6. If the child is correct, let the puppet show the object. Make a big show of praise and encourage the group to applaud. If the child is not correct, let another child help them.
7. Continue to play until everyone has had a turn.

Extending the challenge

- Add some quieter sounds such as rice on a plastic plate, a clock with a softer tick, a mobile phone with the ring-tone turned down or an aerosol air freshener.
- Use a tape recorder or Dictaphone to record some familiar sounds from your setting e.g. taps, a toilet flushing, a phone, the doorbell, the letterbox etc.
- Take photos of the objects too and make the game more independent by leaving the recorder and the photos where children can play together without an adult.

Key words and gestures

- Listen
- Sound
- Recognise
- Turn
- Hide
- Eyes
- Ears
- Choose

Look, listen and note

- *Some children find it really difficult to hear the differences between sound and may find it easier if they close their eyes.*
- *Look for children who are good at listening and make sure you increase the challenge for them by adding more sounds or turning the recorder down low.*
- *Note any unusual responses in children. Young children, especially young boys, may develop 'glue ear' which can affect their hearing and attention.*

Take it outside

- Playing this game outside needs even more concentration to hear sounds over any background noise.
- Record some outdoor sounds to add to your recordings and your games.
- Continue to play 'What can you hear in the garden when you shut your eyes?'

Enhancing the activity

- Use simple musical instruments such as rattles, drums, bells, cymbals, sandpaper blocks and sticks etc.
- Let a child lead the game instead of the 'Talking - Time' puppet'. Play 'I hear with my little ear' by describing something you can hear in the room or outside.

♩ Sing: *We can play on the big bass drum* or *Do your ears hang low?* (Find the words on the Internet).

- Read: *Noisy Town, Noisy Jungle, Noisy Zoo, Noisy Animals* or *Noisy Dinosaurs* (Usborne) *Noisy Fairy Tales* (Ladybird Books) *Noisy Worlds: Jungle, Zoo, Ocean, Night Time* by Maurice Pledger (Templar), *Listen, Listen* by Phillis Gershator, (Barefoot Books).

TOP TIP
Any listening activity will be improved if children touch, wiggle or stroke their ears before they start!

Special names

This core activity is suitable for group time or registration time.

What you need:

Your 'Talking - Time' puppet or a soft toy

A time when children are ready to listen

Enhancing the activity

- If you enjoy puppets, have one on each hand and have a 'Funny name' conversation between them.
- Explore all sorts of names e.g. names for soft toys, characters in stories or brothers and sisters etc.

Their own name is one of the first words children learn to hear and to say. Use this familiarity for some fun games, but be careful not to upset children or offend their sensitivities.

What you do

1 Before you start, make a list of all the children's names and beside each name, add an adjective that is positive and starts with the same sound (i.e. it's alliterative) such as Helpful Hannah, Jazzy Joseph or Smiling Simon. If you run out of adjectives, you can always use the same adjective to describe more than one child.

2 Use the 'Talking-time puppet' to introduce this registration game. It could say 'I know a new way to do the register. It's called Special names. I'll show you how to play it.'

3 Start the register and as you use the 'Talking-time puppet' to say the names, add another word that starts with the same sound, e.g.
Puppet: 'Sunny Sarah, sunny Sarah where are you?'
Child: 'Here I am, here I am, how do you do?
Puppet: 'Lovely Louis, lovely Louis, etc.

4 Try to use positive characteristics.

Extending the challenge

- Try putting two descriptive words in front of each name e.g.} Jazzy jingling Joseph, Lovely laughing Lenny, Busy brave Brenda etc.
- Get the children to choose their own special names.
- Use wordbooks and first dictionaries to find new words to describe yourselves.
- Read: *Mr Tig Tog by Ros Bayley and Lynn Broadbent* (Lawrence Educational Books), *My Book of Rhyming Words and Phrases by Shinobu Akaishi* (Kumon Publishing), *Twinkle, Twinkle Chocolate Bar by John Foster* (OUP) *Oxford First Rhyming Dictionary by John Foster* (OUP).

Look, listen and note

- *Note children who are not able to hear the differences between different versions of even their own names. These children may need more practice with simpler games.*
- *Reward the children who can play the game and praise, but be aware that some children find it difficult.*
- *Make sure the game is not used to tease or hurt anyone's feelings. Make all the adjectives positive by doing your homework before you start!*

Take it outside

- Play the game with object names at clearing up time e.g. 'collect the beautiful bikes, the snaky skipping ropes, the bouncy balls, the blocky bricks.'
- Call children to you by using the new versions of their name e.g. 'Super Sam, I need you here; Marvellous Maddy, do you want to play?'

Key words and gestures

- Mouth
- Name
- Sound
- Different
- Silly
- Funny
- Same
- How many

Involving parents

You could...
- *Share the game with parents, but remind them not to use it to tease or taunt their child, just as a game.*
- *Any use of a child's name in pleasant activities reinforces their knowledge of its sound and their pleasure in hearing parents use it.*
- *Help parents to use their child's name to attract their attention when they want them to listen.*

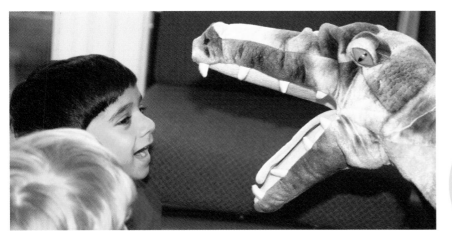

TOP TIP

Say the child's name first when you want them to listen to you, especially when they are absorbed in something else.

I say, you say

This activity is suitable for a group of children.

What you need:

No additional equipment

Enhancing the activity

- Let the children sit facing a friend to copy words and movements.
- Use 'body' and 'mouth' music for sound effects in storytelling.
- Notice and praise any appropriate use of 'body' or 'voice' sounds when children are playing, such as making car or aeroplane noises in play, or talking for puppets and soft toys.
- Try Bobby Shaftoe *Clap Your Hands* by Sue Nicholls (A & C Black), *Bingo Lingo: Supporting Literacy with Songs and Rhymes* by Helen MacGregor (A & C Black) or *The Book of Call and Response: You Sing* by John M. Feierabend (GIA Publications)

Copying and answering another person takes practice, and some children are naturally better at it than others. Play in very small groups first, before asking children to do this complex activity in a larger group where they may have to wait for their turn.

What you do

1 Start off sitting together to explore what you can do with your bodies.
2 Sing or say this simple introductory song (to the tune of Here we go round the Mulberry bush):
   Here we go clapping our two hands,
   Our two hands, our two hands
   Here we go clapping our two hands,
   Early in the morning.
3 Now adapt the rhyme to other body sounds and actions, such as:
   Here we go flicking our two fingers...
   Here we go slapping on our knees...
   Here we go stamping our two feet...
   Here we go patting our fat cheeks...
4 'Body sounds' are an important part of making and listening to different sorts of sounds.
5 After the song, introduce the game 'I say, you say, I do, you do' and let some of the children practise copying what you say, or what you say AND do. In this game, all the children follow your actions and words, not individuals. Here are some examples of things you could do:
   • Say 'clap, clap, clap' as you clap three times.
   • Say 'slap, clap, slap, clap' as you make the movements.
   • Say 'stamp, stamp, stamp, clap, clap, clap' and make the movements.
   • Say 'click, flick, click, flick, click, flick' as you alternately click and flick your fingers.
   • Say 'wave, wave, spin around, wave, wave, spin around, then sit down' as you do this.

Extending the challenge

- Add more 'body sounds' as you think of them, or hear children making them.
- Have a sound parade round the room or the garden.
- Ask the children to suggest sounds and body movements they have invented.

Look, listen and note

- *Look for developing confidence and control over the different parts of children's bodies.*
- *Look for innovative play with body music and sounds, and include these in your sessions.*
- *Note children who have difficulty losing their inhibitions or controlling their enthusiasms!*
- *Listen for children using sounds, as they play out stories of their own.*

Involving parents

You could...
- *Explain to parents that making sounds is part of learning to communicate, and that children really need to be free to make these.*
- *Photograph or film the children doing these games and show the parents.*
- *Have a 'Body Music' show where the children share action songs and movement rhymes with their parents and carers.*

Take it outside

- Take this activity out of doors for some more energetic body music sessions.
- Take a tape recorder or CD player outside for some outdoor action songs.
- Try to lose your inhibitions and use body music and sounds when you play with the children.

TOP TIP
Get some children's CDs that include body music, clapping and other sounds.

Key words and gestures

- Listen
- Watch
- Copy
- Hands
- Body
- Mouth
- Tongue
- Legs
- Sound
- Body music

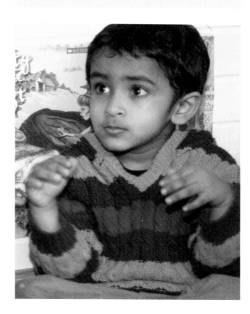

Our kazoo band

This activity is suitable for any number of children.

Kazoos are cheap, great fun and make a really good band! You need a place where the noise won't disturb others! If you haven't got kazoos, you could try making some with cardboard tubes and greaseproof or tracing paper, or combs and paper, but children may find these more difficult to manage.

Enhancing the activity

- Play along to a nursery rhyme CD or familiar music.
- Add some more instruments such as shakers, tambourines, drums or sticks.
- Try: *Kazoo Christmas* by Kickin' Kazoos or *King Kazoo* by Steve Baker (both of which can be downloaded from music sites such as ITunes) or sing songs from *The Handy Band* by Sue Nicholls (A&C Black)
- Read: *The Happy Hedgehog Band* by Martin Waddell (Walker Books) or *Froggy Plays in the Band* by Jonathan London (Puffin Books).

What you do

1 Sit together and let each child take a kazoo.
2 Ask if anyone knows how to play the kazoo, and if they do, let him or her demonstrate.
3 Let the children experiment with the kazoos. They will make a noise, so be prepared!
4 Now ask the children to stop playing while you agree a signal for stopping and starting. This can be a raised or lowered hand, a wand or ribbon stick or a simple instrument such as a drum.
5 Now practise making a tune with the kazoos, 'buzzing' a well-known song together.
6 Once the children can stop and start to your signal, you can have a band session, agreeing the songs before you start.

Key words and gestures

- Sound
- Instrument
- Conductor
- Play
- Stop
- Start
- Blow
- Hum
- Buzz
- Tickle

TOP TIP

Play a variety of music in your setting and encourage children to bring in their favourite songs from home.

Extending the challenge

- Let one child be the conductor.
- Have some children singing while the others accompany them on the kazoos.
- Listen to some pop music that uses kazoos. The chorus of *Roller Coaster* by the Red Hot Chilli Peppers, Crosstown Traffic by Jimi Hendrix and the bands Blind Melon, The Grateful Dead and The Beach Boys all use kazoos in their music.

Involving parents

You could...
- *Show parents how to make simple kazoos at home, by putting some instructions on a card.*
- *You need a cardboard tube from a kitchen roll or toilet paper, some greaseproof or tracing paper and an elastic band. Cut some paper big enough to cover the end of the tube, and fix it on with the elastic band. Make a small hole near the top end of the tube, then hum or buzz into the open end of the tube. The paper will vibrate to make the sound.*

Take it outside

- Take your band out of doors where you can make even more noise!
- Use some ribbon sticks, flags and other decorations for a marching band.
- Invite some of the other children in your setting to join your band and participate in the fun.

Look, listen and note

- *Watch how children manage the stopping and starting involved.*
- *Look for children who really can't manage this activity*
- *Listen for children who can sing in tune. This is a real indication of early language experts and good listening skills.*
- *Note those children who can march and play at the same time. This indicates good development of physical skills.*

Body sound patterns

This activity is suitable for any number of children.

What you need:

A space

Enhancing the activity

- Add some simple instruments such as shakers or sticks so that some children can play instruments and others can contribute with body music.

- ♪ Make a body music accompaniment to a nursery rhyme CD.
- ♪ Sing along to *Singable Songs for the Very Young* by Raffi or *Count with Keeping the Beat* from www.keepingthebeat.co.uk or *Let's Go, Zudie-o* by Helen MacGregor (A & C Black)

- Read: *Making Sounds* by Charlotte Guillain (Heinemann), *The Happy Hedgehog Band* by Martin Waddell (Walker Books)

Making 'body music' is popular with children and needs no preparation! Children love exploring the sounds they can make, and whole body moment helps rhythm and beat, essential for fluency in reading and speaking.

What you do

1 Sit together and remind children of all the different sounds they can make with their bodies:
  - Clapping their hands
  - Slapping their thighs or legs
  - 'Popping' their cheeks with their finger
  - Humming and buzzing
  - Clicking with their fingers and their tongues
  - Stamping
2 Practise all these together, then ask the children to show you their best sound.
3 Now play 'I say, you do' – you say a pattern and the children do it back to you. Make these first patterns simple and watch to be sure they can all do them back.
4 When the children have played 'I say, you do' you can put together some simple sequences of sounds, and say them as you do them:
  - Stamp, stamp, clap, clap, stamp, stamp, stamp
  - Click, slap, click, slap, clap, clap, clap
  - Stamp and clap, stamp and clap, click, click, click, and pop.

Look, listen and note

- *Note children who have a really good sense of beat and rhythm. They will enjoy being leaders and conductors.*
- *Look for children who find it difficult to stop once they have started or lose control. Give these children more individual attention and praise for getting it right.*
- *Watch for children who still find the co-ordination difficult.*

Key words and gestures

- Body
- Hands
- Clap
- Together
- Beat
- In time
- Accompany
- Conductor

TOP TIP

Clapping or slapping on opposite sides of the body strengthens links in the brain.

Involving parents

You could...
- *Explain to parents that making body sounds is a useful skill, not just an irritating habit! Encourage them to join in with appropriate sound making.*
- *Make a video of the children in their band, so parents can see the value of this activity in helping co-ordination.*

Extending the challenge

- Have some children sing while the others accompany them with body music.
- Play clapping games every day — in spare moments, just for fun.

Take it outside

- Take your body band out of doors where you can move more easily.
- Invite some of the other children in your setting or school to join the 'Brilliant Body Band' and join in the fun.

Tap that name

This core activity is suitable for a small group of children.

What you need:

A shallow basket for your instruments

Some 'found' or home made instruments such as matching pairs of coloured wooden bricks, tops from fabric softener bottles or large aerosols, chopsticks, kitchen roll tubes or sticks from the garden

Some simple musical instruments such as claves, drums, tambourines, woodblocks, castanets and triangles

You could ask a friendly carpenter or a parent to make some pairs of wooden shapes such as fish or birds to tap together.

Un-pitched instruments such as sticks and blocks are very useful for establishing simple rhythmic ability. Children need lots of practice in these simple activities that underpin the development of language and literacy.

What you do

1 Talk about where you might hear tapping sounds such as someone knocking on your door, footsteps, a branch tapping the window, a bird pecking, hammering or feet tapping to music.
2 Give each child a small stick or a chopstick and walk around your room together making gentle tapping sounds on surfaces and objects. Make sure that they follow this rule: 'Gently tap yourself or things, not people!'
3 Ask the children to take turns tapping different surfaces and objects, and listen to their sounds. How do the sounds vary?
4 Now sit together and use one finger to tap a simple pattern on the palm of the other hand.
5 Help children to tap or clap the rhythm of their name e.g. John (1 tap), Megan (2 taps), Oliver (3 taps).
6 Now look together at the basket of instruments. Let the children choose pairs and experiment with them.
7 Take turns in tapping names with the instruments – the child taps their name, then everyone copies them.

Key words and gestures

- Listen
- Copy
- Tap
- Gently
- Same
- Different
- Sound
- Loud
- Soft

TOP TIP
Use plastic plates or cheap washing up bowls with garden sticks or chopsticks to keep a beat.

Look, listen and note

- A sense of rhythm and beat is an early indicator of readiness to read, so watch for this ability emerging.
- Note those children who still can't bring their hands together evenly to make a sound.
- Make a note of any children who can't keep a beat or copy a pattern. These children may need more practice in smaller groups.

Enhancing the activity

- Make and play home made 'tappers' using pairs of wooden bricks, plastic tops and lids, wooden sticks or empty plastic boxes and cardboard snack tubes.
- Design drums using different sized wide-mouthed containers. Make the skin by stretching a deflated balloon over the opening and fastening with rubber bands.
- Good CDs for beat work include *Keeping the Beat* and *Keeping the Beat Counting* from www.keepingthebeat.co.uk and *Beat Baby* and Beat *Baby Raps* from www.

Take it outside

- Use sticks and other simple instruments to tap and beat on drainpipes, railings, fences, climbing apparatus or doors.
- Offer baskets of instruments for free choice play out of doors.
- On dry days have a music session with a tape recorder or CD player out of doors.

Extending the challenge

- Let children tap the names of their friends for others to guess. They tap the name and that child should stand up. This will create a good discussion because some names have the same number of taps (or syllables)!
- Use the pairs of 'tappers' to play 'Tap that tune'. Children tap a favourite tune and the others must guess the tune.
- Tap along to simple songs on CD or the radio.

Involving parents

You could...
- *Encourage parents to use home made sound makers such as cutlery, sticks or other items to make a 'band' at home.*
- *Take photos of children using simple resources such as boxes, chopsticks, and wooden bricks.*
- *Help parents to understand how important a sense of beat is in learning to read.*

Karaoke

This core activity is suitable for any number of children.

What you need:

A simple children's tape recorder/CD player with a microphone, or a children's karaoke machine

A quiet place to record

A place for noise for the karaoke sessions!

Enhancing the activity

- Try adding other simple recording devices such as 'Talking Tins', 'Talking Photo Frames' (where children can record their own comments to accompany photos and pictures), or 'Talking Postcards'.
- Encourage children to record each other talking and singing.
- Try a children's 'Dance Mat' for moving and singing together.
- Try *Music Express Foundation Stage* by Sue Nicholls (A & C Black) or *Whole World* by Christopher Corr (Barefoot Books).

Karaoke is great fun, either as a group or as a self-chosen activity. It's even more fun if you can record your own songs to play back and sing along to afterwards.

What you do

1 If the children have not used a karaoke machine or recorder, you need to explain how your model works and let the children experiment with it.
2 Now you can get involved in a range of activities such as:
   - Singing along to CDs of simple songs and tunes (either nursery rhymes or popular songs);
   - Recording yourselves singing, then singing along with your own recordings;
   - Offering opportunities for children to sing alone or in pairs or groups, recording themselves then singing along;
   - Downloading tunes from the internet to use for singing;
   - Making your own recordings of rhythm and instruments to sing to.
3 The children will need help at first, but they will soon get the idea and may well prove to be more ingenious and creative than you expect!

Take it outside

- Look for all weather wireless CD players that can safely be used out of doors.
- Make a karaoke place in your shed or store, where the children can make a stage, sing and listen to each other.

Extending the challenge

- Try recording interviews or making simple PowerPoint presentations of singing and recording activities.
- Use simple video cameras to record karaoke sessions and other singing and music activities.
- Let children make up their own songs and musical accompaniments, and record these on tape or video.

Look, listen and note

- *Some children really enjoy karaoke. Make sure they have plenty of opportunities but don't let them take over!*
- *Shy children may not like to join in, but may want to have a go in a less exposed situation, such as with one other friend.*
- *Watch for children who can sing in tune at this age. This is a real indication of their ability to hear pitch.*
- *Look for difficulties when following a familiar tune.*

Key words and gestures

- Listen
- Join in
- Together
- Favourite
- Record
- Songs
- Music

TOP TIP

The Easi-Speak microphone from TTS is a children's microphone that records as you sing into it!

Involving parents

You could...
- *Suggest that family karaoke is a good idea, but only if parents enjoy it.*
- *Sing-along CDs are very good for car journeys and make the time go much more quickly. Have a sheet of recommended CDs available for parents.*

Tape recorder fun

This core activity is suitable for any number of children.

What you need:

A simple children's tape recorder/CD player with a microphone, or a Dictaphone

A quiet place to record and play back recordings

Enhancing the activity

- Take photos of the objects and events the children record and use these to build up sequences.
- Use 'Talking Tins' (from www.talkingproducts.co.uk). They are simple recording devices that have 30 second of recording time – enough for just a sentence or one instruction. Record an idea, an instruction or some information and leave them near activities such as sand, bricks or water play.

TOP TIP
Remember girls usually have better hearing than boys and may find loud noises stressful.

Build on the karaoke activity by having some more fun with tape recorders or Dictaphones. Listening to their own and others' voices is an activity that children really enjoy.

What you do

1 It is never too early to help children to learn about how ICT resources work. Make sure you show them how each piece of equipment works and then let children have plenty of practice in free play.
2 Now you can get involved in a range of recording activities such as these:
   - Record sounds in the environment and play 'What was that?' Children record sounds around the room or the building, then they play them back for their friends to guess. Children may need some help from an adult as they get used to the recording process.
   - Let the children record themselves talking or singing and play 'Who was that?' in a group.
   - Record short sequences of sounds such as a key turning, a door opening, footsteps, then the door closing; or a car door opening and closing, the car starting and driving away; children coming in from play, sitting down, singing or having snack; turning on the tap, washing up, drying dishes, letting the water out and putting dishes away.
   - Let children take simple recorders home to record what happens there, then play it back for the rest of the group.
   - On Monday, leave the recorder in the quiet area, invite children to record their news during the day and to play the 'Today's News' bulletin back at the end of the day.
3 Once children get used to the recording process, they will have great fun finding mystery sounds for their friends.

Take it outside

- Encourage children to use recording equipment out of doors to record the natural and man-made environment.
- Use 'Talking Tins' out of doors for ideas and suggestions.
- Take a tape recorder with you on local visits and outings so you can record the sounds of the experience. This will make recall and memories stronger and easier to access.

Look, listen and note

- *Watch for children who have a real technological interest and ability, and use this as a trigger for other areas of learning.*
- *Note the children who have most difficulty in hearing and differentiating between sounds. These children may need additional activities in very small groups.*
- *Observe children in different weathers and seasons. Many children have better sensory perception in the spring and on sunny days!*

Extending the challenge

- When you have recorded some sounds, play them back with the volume turned down so children have to really listen carefully.
- Show the children how to use 'Talking Tins' and let them record messages and instructions for their friends.
- Use a simple video recorder to record objects and sounds together. Try getting very near an object that makes a sound, and then play a guessing game to find out what it is.
- Read: *First Picture Trucks, Building Site, Town: with sounds* by Felicity Brooks (Usborne), *Boom Boom, Beep Beep, Roar!* by David Diehl (Stirling).

Involving parents

You could...
- *Suggest some simple sound games to play at home.*
- *Encourage parents to help their children with listening skills by concentrating on and talking about sounds in the home and in the community.*
- *Offer some simple photo cards for listening activities.*

Key words and gestures

- Record
- Loud
- Soft
- Volume
- Recognise
- Difficult
- Controls
- Play back

Follow the pattern

This core activity is suitable for any number of children.

What you need:

No special equipment

A quiet and comfortable place to be together

Enhancing the activity

- Use a 'Talking - Time' puppet (preferably with hands) to help the children with the steady beat.
- Keep a nursery rhyme book handy so you always have a rhyme ready for these activities.
- Clap in a steady beat to the radio or a CD. Use lots of different sorts and styles of music.
- Books for inspiration include:
- Kids Make Music: Clapping and Tapping from Bach to Rock by Avery Hart (Williamson Publishing)
- OThe Book of Tapping and Clapping by John M. Feierabend (GIA Publications)
- OBeat Baby and Beat Baby Rhymes and Raps by Ros www.

'Steady beat' or 'Beat competency' is a key skill, not just for moving, but also for motor control and all areas of learning. Clapping is the first and most lasting way of developing a sense of beat that is essential for learning to read. Steady beat is not the same as rhythm! These activities don't need any resources and can be done at any time when you have a few spare minutes, as well as during planned group sessions.

What you do

1   Spend plenty of time exploring steady beat sounds and movements as you sing, move or listen to music. These can include:
    - *Clapping;*
    - *Patting or slapping hands on knees, shoulders or heads;*
    - *Tapping one finger on the palm of the other hand;*
    - *Stamping with alternate feet;*
    - *Marching;*
    - *Playing simple instruments such as chopsticks.*
2   Move in steady beat:
    - *When you run, walk, stamp, march;*
    - *Sing action songs and rhymes;*
    - *Say nursery rhymes together;*
    - *Count or sing counting songs.*
3   Or you could make up some songs with steady beat words that describe the movements. Here are some examples that use the movements in the list above:
    Slap and clap, slap and clap
    Slap and clap, slap and clap
    We can slap and clap, can you?
    Clap like us, slap like us
    You can do it too!

Take it outside

- Steady beat work is great for outdoor learning, both in free play and outdoor group time.
- Watch the children and pick up on their rhythmical movements. Incorporate these in your sessions.
- Organise a parade with flag or banners to wave and musical instruments to play as you march along.

Look, listen and note

- *Some children find maintaining a steady beat very difficult. Note these children and give them a bit more help in smaller groups.*
- *Other children will be able to maintain a beat easily, even when singing, playing an instrument or waving a flag. Make sure you give these children plenty of practice as they move towards reading and writing skills.*
- *Provide musical instruments and watch how children use them in free play.*

Involving parents

You could...
- *Encourage parents to play clapping games at home – the more they do it, the better their child will get!*
- *Have some tapes or CDs of music with a strong beat for families to borrow and play at home.*

Key words and gestures

- Clap
- Stamp
- Listen
- Follow
- Same
- Steady
- Keep going
- Sing
- Say
- Words
- Movements

Extending the challenge

- Once the children have mastered the steadiness of the beat, incorporate more movements.
- Do the rhymes on the move, walking or marching in time to the steady beat.
- Play simple percussion instruments that are in pairs, such as sticks, bricks, blocks, pencils or chopsticks. Extend this work by offering a plastic plate and a stick to each child.

TOP TIP

'Steady beat' is like a heartbeat, rhythmical and steady, not following the words or rhythm of a song.

39

Make and shake

This activity is suitable for small groups of children.

What you need:

A range of recycled, 'found' and bargain materials for instruments such as boxes, plastic containers, yogurt pots, tins, cardboard tubes, plastic bottles of all sizes, snack and sweet tubes, plastic caps and tops, small bells, paper and plastic, sticks, plastic and paper plates

Lentils, dried beans, beads, gravel and small dry pasta shapes

Masking and 'duct' tape, glue sticks, elastic bands, string and wool

Strong glue (adult only)

Take it outside

- Play some music out of doors. You can make a really big noise outside!
- Collect seeds, nuts, cones and sticks for making instruments.
- Hang some musical instruments outside so children can help themselves to one and play an impromptu tune.

Making simple instruments is a great way to involve children in listening to and making sounds. Here are some more complex instruments to add to the simple ones described in Sounds Fun 30-50 months. Once you have made the instruments in small groups, you can have a band of any size.

What you do

1. Collect the resources and make sure they are clean and hygienic (consult your Health and Safety policy for guidance on using recycled materials).
2. Look at the resources with the children and explain that you are going to make some musical instruments for a band. Ask them how you could make something that makes sounds, using the materials they can see. Welcome all suggestions, and encourage them to think of shakers, tappers, bangers, stringed instruments etc.
3. If the children have difficulty thinking of something to make, put 'home-made musical instruments' in a search engine and you'll find lots of ideas.
4. Now help the children to make their musical instruments. Older children could draw a plan first. Be available to support them through the tricky bits but try not to interfere with their experiments.
5. Children could decorate their musical instrument with felt pens or paint, when they are happy with it.
6. When everyone has made an instrument, let each child introduce their creation to the rest of the group, including giving it a name and demonstrating the sound it makes.
7. Now practise using the instruments in a band or to accompany songs and rhymes.

Extending the challenge

- Keep talking about the instruments and give children opportunities to improve on or re-make their own creations.
- Set some challenges such as making a guitar or a big drum.
- In pairs, the children could teach each other how to play their instruments.

Key words and gestures

- Make
- Try
- Fix
- Design
- Listen
- Sound

- Play
- Fingers
- Band
- Conduct
- Together

TOP TIP

Cheap plastic washing up bowls make great drums. Add some mops for drumsticks.

Enhancing the activity

- Provide some books or pictures to inspire the creations. Don't make the challenge too difficult!
- You could add some ready-made instruments to your band, and compare the sounds and shapes.
- See if you can find some music played on home made instruments, or record and listen to your own band.

Try: *Make Music!* by Julia Lawson (Evans Brothers), *Pat a Cake, Make and Shake: Make and Play Your Own Musical Instruments* by Sue Nicholls (A&C Black) for more instructions on making simple instruments or *The Little Book of Junk Music* by Simon G.G. Macdonald (A & C Black/Featherstone).

Involving parents

You could...
- *Produce a take-home sheet for parents to help them make simple instruments with their children: shakers, simple drums etc.*
- *Make a display of familiar objects that can be used to make music: saucepans, wooden spoons, biscuit tins, plastic bowls and boxes etc.*
- *Offer some CDs of unusual music to borrow such as the junk music band Stomp.*

Look, listen and note

- *Use this activity to observe creative and hand control skills.*
- *Watch for technological ability as well as creative ability and good listening.*
- *If younger children have difficulty using the instruments, hold their hands gently in yours as you play.*
- *Watch for children who have a well-developed sense of rhythm and beat or those that can sing and play together without adult help.*

Find a rhyming friend

This activity is suitable for a group of children (even number).

What you need:

Objects or pictures of objects in rhyming pairs – enough for one object or picture per child. Some examples of pairs are: hen/pen mouse/house frog/dog pear/bear car/star sink/pink rat/hat cup/pup sea/pea coat/boat fish/dish brick/stick ham/jam bell/shell sun/bun fox/socks etc.

A basket or box for the objects or picture cards.

A big space to run around

First rhyming activities work well if they are active. Some children develop an understanding of rhyme from a very early age while others find it really difficult. This activity will keep them on the move as they learn.

What you do

1 Sit together and then tip the objects/pictures out of the basket and look at them. Make sure all the children know the names of all the objects.
2 Explain the game. Each child has a rhyming object/picture and must run around saying its name until they find the child with the matching rhyming object/picture.
3 Now put all the objects/pictures back in the basket. Hold the basket up high and let each child pick a card or object without seeing what it is. Give a moment for any queries or children looking confused!
4 When you say 'Go' the children run all over the space, saying the name of the object they have. When they find their matching rhyme partner, they sit down and wait until everyone has finished.
5 The pairs of children hold up their objects and say the rhyming words to the rest of the group

Involving parents

You could...
- Produce a take-home sheet for parents with rhyming pairs of pictures so they can make their own game to play.
- Remind parents of the rhyming songs they know.
- Add some rhyming storybooks to your book loan collection. Ask your local librarian to help you with titles.

Look, listen and note

- *Some children will love this game, and may play it independently. Make sure these children have plenty of challenging follow-up activities.*
- *Note those children who find rhyming difficult or can't find a match through the sound. They may need more practice at a simple level.*
- *Watch for children who are confused by this sort of game and give them practice in even smaller groups.*

Take it outside

- Sing rhyming songs outside when you are playing.
- Take group times outside occaionaly – 'Find a rhyming friend' is a good one to use.
- Hide the rhyming objects or pictures outside and have a rhyming treasure hunt.

Enhancing the activity

- Add more rhyming pairs as you think of them.
- Use clip art or magazine and catalogue pictures for more pairs.
- See if you can find some music played on home made instruments or record and listen to your own band.

♪ *Make Music!* by Julia Lawson, Evans Brothers
♪ Try '*Pat a Cake, Make and Shake*': *Make and Play Your Own Musical Instruments*, by Sue Nicholls; (A&C Black) for more instructions on making simple instruments.
The Little Book of Junk Music: by Simon G.G. Macdonald; (A & C Black/Featherstone)

Key words and gestures

- Make
- Try
- Fix
- Design
- Listen
- Sound
- Play
- Fingers
- Band
- Conduct
- Together

Extending the challenge

- Keep talking about the instruments and give children opportunities to improve on or re-make their own creations.
- Set some challenges such as making a guitar or a big drum.
- In pairs, the children could teach each other how to play their instruments.

TOP TIP

Keep a list of rhymes for future reference and add more pairs as you think of them!

Repetitive rhymes

This activity is suitable for a group of children.

What you need:

A big space

Enhancing the activity

- Add more body parts and actions to make more verses.
- Make some simple sailor hats to wear.
- Sing the song in half groups with an audience.

♩ Sing other songs with actions: *One finger, one thumb keep moving; Heads, shoulders, knees and toes* or *Wind the bobbin up.*

♩ For more rhyming games and activities refer to *The Little Book of Games with Sounds* by Sally

TOP TIP
Make a songbook and keep it handy to remind you of words and actions.

Repetitive rhymes with actions are popular and useful for practising rhyme and rhythm together. Make a collection of these and keep them handy so you can use them at group times and in odd moments.

What you do

1 This rhyme has actions and here are the words:
A sailor went to sea, sea, sea (hand drawing waves)
To see what he could see, see, see (look through a telescope)
But all that he could see, see, see (hand shading eyes)
Was the bottom of the deep blue sea, sea, sea. (bend knees and wriggle down into the sea)

A sailor went to sea, chop, chop (hand drawing waves, then chop twice with side of hand)
To see what he could see, chop, chop, (telescope, then chop twice with side of hand)
But all that he could see, chop, chop (hand shading eyes, then chop twice with side of hand)
Was the bottom of the deep blue sea, chop, chop (wriggle down, then chop twice with side of hand)

A sailor went to sea, chop, knee (hand drawing waves, chop once with side of hand, tap knee)
To see what he could see, chop, knee (telescope, chop once with side of hand, tap knee)
But all that he could see, chop, knee (hand shading eyes, chop once with side of hand, tap knee)
Was the bottom of the deep blue sea, chop, knee (wriggle down, chop , tap knee)

Extending the challenge

- See if you can sing the song faster, without getting in a muddle.
- Make your own rhyming songs – as you see, it doesn't matter if they don't make sense!
- Teach one group, then get them to teach others – a real skill.

Look, listen and note

- *Watch for children who can't move and sing at the same time! They may need some extra help and practice.*
- *Look for leaders in these games i.e. the children who learn the songs and actions quickly and can even teach them to other children.*
- *You may find some children are embarrassed about these games, where failure is a possibility. Give these children practice in smaller groups where they feel more confident or let them just watch until they feel like joining in.*

Key words and gestures

- Rhyme
- Movement
- Action
- Together
- Turn
- In order
- Sense
- Nonsense

Take it outside

- Action rhymes are very good activities for out of doors, when you are in your outdoor area, at the park or in the woods.
- Make up silly movement songs with nonsense words and sing these out of doors where you can make as much noise and move around as much as you like.

Involving parents

You could...
- *Make a video of the children singing this song so parents can learn it too.*
- *Ask parents to tell you about rhyming songs they remember singing when they were children.*
- *Add some books or CDs of rhymes and songs to your loan collection. Ask your local librarian to help you with titles or use the Internet.*

Goldilocks

This activity is suitable for groups of children.

What you need:

A book version of *Goldilocks and the Three Bears*

Three bowls, three spoons, three chairs, three beds (or blankets/ sleeping bags) – in three different sizes

Involving parents

You could...
- *Make a video of the children singing this story so parents can learn it too.*
- *Offer some simple story bags for home use. Don't make them too complicated and remember to add the story or the song words too.*
- *Add some books or CDs of story songs to your loan collection.*

Some rhymes have real potential for follow up activities with masks, props and costumes that give children practice in recall, rhyme and story telling in role. Try this one and then make some prop boxes or bags for other rhyming stories so you can use them in group work, 'Talking Times' or for independent play.

What you do

1 This is the rhyme about Goldilocks, which has simple actions. Here are the words, you could look on Youtube.com for examples of children singing and doing the actions:
When Goldilocks went to the house of the bears
Oh, what did her blue eyes see? (put fingers round eyes like glasses)
A bowl that was huge and a bowl that was small, (draw each bowl as you sing)
A bowl that was tiny and that was all.
She counted them – one, two, three (point or show fingers, 1, 2, 3)

When Goldilocks went to the house of the bears
Oh, what did her blue eyes see?
A chair that was huge and a chair that was small, (draw each chair as you sing)
And a chair that was tiny and that was all.
She counted them - one, two, three. (point or show fingers, 1, 2, 3)

When Goldilocks went to the house of the bears
Oh, what did her blue eyes see?
A bed that was huge and a bed that was small, (draw each bed as you sing)
And a bed that was tiny and that was all.
She counted them - one, two, three. (point or show fingers, 1, 2, 3)

When Goldilocks went to the house of the bears
Oh, what did her blue eyes see?
A bear that was huge and a bear that was small,
And a bear that was tiny and that was all.
They growled at her - one, two, three! (growl three times, getting louder each time)

2 Sing the song through with the children first to familiarise them with the order and the words.
3 Now look at the props you have collected and sing the song again, using or pointing to the props at the appropriate parts of the song.

Look, listen and note

- *Let confident children have a go at leading and watch how they do.*
- *Watch for children who get lost in the song or who can't move and sing at the same time! They may need some extra help and practice.*
- *Action games bring out the best in some children, even those who are less confident. Watch for these children and continue to use role-play as a vehicle for learning.*

Key words and gestures

- Rhyme
- Movement
- Action
- Count
- Point
- Together
- Eyes
- Listen

Take it outside

- These activities with prop boxes or bags are great for outdoor play, where children can use them in free choice, practising the stories and making up new versions.
- It's a good idea to do 'Talking Time' or small group activities out of doors sometimes. Some children really do learn better outside!

Extending the challenge

- Take photos and make the song into a storybook for children to read.
- Play some rhyming games with the words in the song: bear/pear/pair/hair/where, eyes/size/guys/lies/prize etc.
- Let one of the more confident children lead a singing session instead of an adult, but stay near to help if they get stuck or lose their nerve.

Enhancing the activity

- Add some ears on headbands and a golden wig for Goldilocks so children can walk through the story as you sing it.
- Leave the resources in your role-play area so children can play the song again by themselves.
- Use your role-play house for the story, setting out the table and the other objects.
- Sing other songs with actions such as Little Rabbit FooFoo, If you're happy and you know it, There were ten in the bed, There was a princess long ago or Miss Polly had a dolly.
- Read Goldilocks and the Three Bears, The three little pigs, Red Riding Hood and other traditional tales – all with CD, by Estelle Corke (Child's Play International) or *Goldilocks and the Three Bears* by John Kurtz (Jump at the Sun) – one of a series with multicultural characters.

TOP TIP
Use search engines such as Google to find the words to any song you need.

Ring games

This activity is suitable for a group of children.

Enhancing the activity

- Add some simple costumes or props for the characters.
- Leave the props in your role-play area so children can play the song again by themselves.
- Turn your role-play area into a castle or palace for retelling traditional or modern stories.
- Refer to books such as *Oranges and Lemons: Singing and Dancing Games* by Karen King (OUP), *This Little Puffin: the classis collection of Nursery Rhymes* by Elizabeth Matterson (Puffin Books) or *Bobby Shaftoe Clap Your Hands* by Sue Nicholls (A & C Black).

Sing other ring games with actions such as *The farmer's in his den, In and out the dust bluebells, Sandy girl, Oranges and lemons* or *Here we go Looby Lou.*

Ring games give more opportunities for singing, rhyming, moving and listening. This is just one example of a ring game with a story. Some have more repetition and rhyme than others. Singing and remembering a wide range of ring games is a real advantage to children as they begin to tell and invent their own stories and rhymes.

What you do

1 This is a very well-known ring game with characters. It is based on the Sleeping Beauty story which many children will already know. Here are the words and actions:
   There was a princess, long ago, long ago, long ago;
   There was a princess long ago, long, long ago.
   (The princess stands in middle, others stand in a ring with hands joined)

   And she lived in a big high tower, a big high tower, a big high tower;
   And she lived in a big high tower, long, long ago.
   (Children raise their joined hands to make a tower)

   A wicked fairy cast a spell, cast a spell, cast a spell;
   A wicked fairy cast a spell, long, long ago.
   (The wicked fairy creeps round and into the circle to cast the spell)

   The princess slept for a hundred years, a hundred years, a hundred years;
   (The princess falls down asleep in the circle)

   A great big forest grew around, grew around, grew around;
   (Children raise their joined hands to shoulder height as the forest)

   A handsome prince came riding by, riding by, riding by;
   (The prince gallops round the outside of the circle)

   He took his sword and chopped it down, chopped it down, chopped it down,
   (The prince 'chops' the forest of arms down)

   He took her hand to wake her up, wake her up, wake her up,,
   (The prince wakes princess)

   Everybody's happy now, happy now, happy now;
   So everybody's happy now, happy now.

Look, listen and note

- *Action games bring out the best in some children. Sometimes those who are less confident find being in character liberating. Watch for these children and continue to use role-play as a vehicle for learning.*
- *Watch for children who really enjoy ring games and encourage them to ask their friends to join in.*

Key words and gestures

- Ring
- Character
- Move
- Action
- Sing
- Together
- Long ago
- Story
- Song

Extending the challenge

- Take photos and make the song into a storybook for children to read.
- Add more ring games to the children's repertoire.
- Make links between these ring games and the stories they are based on.

Take it outside

- Sing ring games out of doors. Get together informally with a group of children or make it a 'small group time' with your key children.
- Hang some rhyming pairs of pictures or picture clues to songs and stories on elastic from bushes and trees.

TOP TIP
The internet is a great place to find new songs, words to old ones and follow up activities.

Involving parents

You could...
- *Take some photos of the children playing ring games so parents can see what happens and watch their own child's response.*
- *Add some books or CDs of story songs to your loan collection.*

Jelly on a plate

This activity is suitable for a group of children.

What you need:

A big space to move around, indoors or outside

Enhancing the activity

- Play with a series of photos of the different foods. Put the photos face down on the floor and turn them over one at a time for a different version of the song.
- Have real food, or replicas made from dough, to help the children with the order and sound of the different foods.

♪ Sing other songs about food such as *Hot cross buns*, *Mix a pancake*, *Sing a song of sixpence*, *Pease porridge hot* or *Five fat sausages*.

♪ Share some poems from *Tasty Poems* by Jill Bennett (OUP) or *What's on the menu? Food Poems* by Bobby S. Goldstein (Puffin Books).

TOP TIP
Remember that some children can hear better if they close or cover their eyes.

There are lots of rhymes and songs about food. Here are some suggestions for using them in 'Talking Time' or other language sessions. The familiar rhyme suggested here helps with alliteration (similar sounds) and rhymes. Children love talking and singing about food.

What you do

1 This song is both popular and familiar and gives you a starter for some work on sounds and rhymes.
Jelly on a plate, jelly on a plate
Wibble wobble, wibble wobble, jelly on a plate

Sausage in a pan, sausage in a pan
Sizzle sizzle, sizzle sizzle, sizzle sizzle bang!

Noodles on a fork, noodles on a fork
Twirly wirly, twirly wirly, noodles on a fork

Popcorn in a pot, popcorn in a pot
Popping popping, never stopping, popcorn in a pot

Honey on a spoon, honey on a spoon
Runny honey, runny honey, honey on a spoon

Jelly on a plate, jelly on a plate
Wibble wobble, wibble wobble, jelly on a plate.

2 Stand or sit in a circle as you sing the song, doing the actions for each verse.

Take it outside

- Use dough to make food out of doors and sing as you work.
- Make some really big sound matching dominoes or cards and play a sound game outside on a big scale.

Key words and gestures

- Rhyme
- Sound
- Food
- Favourite
- New
- Version
- Sound
- Same
- Letter

Look, listen and note

- *Children love food. Watch the children who are particularly switched on by these poems and songs.*
- *Note those children who really enjoy listening games and finding matching games. These children may become early readers.*
- *Some children can't hear sound differences very well. Watch these children closely to see if they need a hearing check.*

Involving parents

You could...
- *Provide some sheets of 'sounds the same' pictures for parents to use in games at home.*
- *Encourage parents to enjoy nonsense rhymes and poems with their children.*
- *Add some poetry books to your home reading collection.*

Extending the challenge

- Add some more foods and alliterative sounds, such as:
  - Apple in the bowl, apple in the bowl, round and rosy, round and rosy, apple in the bowl.
  - Sandwich in the box, sandwich in the box, cheese for chomping, cheese for chomping, sandwich in the box.
  - Cornflakes in a bowl, cornflakes in a bowl, crisp and crunchy, crisp and crunchy, cornflakes in a bowl.
  - Porridge in a pan, porridge in a pan, stir it, spoon it, stir it, spoon it, porridge in a pan.
  - Ice cubes in my drink, ice cubes in my drink, clink and clatter, clink and clatter, ice cubes in my drink.

On the washing line

This core activity is suitable for a group of children.

What you need:

Some pairs or trios of objects that start with the same sound, such as: peg/pen/pig/penny, button/ball/brick/bead, sock/scissors/soap, ring/rubber/rabbit. Make sure the objects really do start with the same sound, not just the same letter, and concentrate on consonants to start with, not vowels which are more difficult.

Some objects without sound pairs

A washing line, pegs and some transparent plastic sandwich bags

A basket

Take it outside

- When you are outside, say the rhyme as you look at objects and people – 'It's Mark, it's Mark, it's M-M-Mark.'
- Put up a washing line outside or take some bags on a walk and collect natural objects that start with the same sound in the same bag.

By the time they reach Reception many children can isolate the initial sound of a word and match it with other words that start with the same sound. Start with some simple matches and gradually make it more complex by adding more sounds and more matches of the same sound.

What you do

1 Peg the line up near where you are going to sit and at a height that children can reach.
2 Peg some bags on the line.
3 Put all the objects in a basket·and sit in a circle, somewhere quiet.
4 Sing a simple rhyme as you take each object out of the basket and pass it round. Say: *'What's this? Yes...*
   It's a ring, it's a ring, it's a r-r-ring
   Here it comes, here it comes ring, ring, ring'
   As you pass the ring round the circle.
5 Put the ring in the middle of the circle and take another object from the basket, or let a child choose one.
6 When you have taken all the objects out of the basket, including the odd ones out, ask the children if they can find two objects that sound the same.
7 When the children have found a matching pair, say, for example, s-s-sock, s-s-scissors together as they put each one in one of the bags on the line.
8 Give plenty of praise for listening and matching the sounds.
9 Continue with the game, taking turns to choose matching pairs and putting them in a separate bag for each sound.
10 At the end, you will have some objects left. Talk about the ones that can go in bags with the pairs you have already matched.
11 When you only have the 'odd' objects left in the basket, say their names and talk about why they can't go on the line.

Key words and gestures

- Same
- Different
- Sound
- Pair
- Listen
- Letter
- Carefully
- Choose

Look, listen and note

- *Look for children who are already able to hear the similarities and differences between initial sounds. They may need a more challenging collection of objects.*
- *Some children may still have difficulty hearing initial sounds even in a singe word or name of an object. Give these children plenty of practice in simple listening activities.*
- *Note the children who still confuse sounds or are using baby talk. This is a cause for concern by this age, so talk to parents and get some advice.*

Extending the challenge

- Once you are sure they can differentiate between the initial sounds, add some more complex sounds such as ch, sh, th.
- Start a notebook in your room with a page for each letter of the alphabet. When you think of new words, add them to save everyone time! Gradually work through the initial consonants, giving plenty of repetition of each one.
- As you put objects in the bags, write the initial letter on the bag or a piece of

TOP TIP

Collect items that start with common sounds so you have a bag or box for each of the common sounds in your cupboard. This will save you lots of time!

Enhancing the activity

- Add some pictures of objects as well as objects themselves.
- Use small world animals and characters as well as the usual pieces of equipment. Spiderman and Superman may well switch on this game for some boys!
- *The Little Book of Washing Lines* (Featherstone/A &C Black) has lots more ideas for activities using pegs and lines.
- Share *Phonic Stories for Young Readers*, a series of six titles by Phil Roxbee Cox (Usborne)

Involving parents

You could...
- *Give parents ideas of simple objects such as snake, sock and spoon, that they could use for the same sort of sounding rhymes at home.*
- *Bedtime and getting dressed are good times for practising sounds. Help parents to talk their child through dressing by saying things such as 'You need a s-s-sock next' or 'Now take off your t-t-teeshirt'.*

I went to the zoo...

This core activity is suitable for a group of children.

This activity builds on earlier work on alliteration – recognising and repeating the same sound. It also uses a familiar song. This helps children to join in even if they are at an early stage of recognising similar sounds.

What you do

1 Sit in a circle and explain what you are going to do.
2 Say 'This game is called 'I went to the zoo and I saw...' and this is how we play it. I will take an animal out of the bag and we will think of a word that describes it.
3 Take an animal out of the bag and talk about a brown bear, a lumpy lion, a zingy zebra etc. As children get used to the idea, let them suggest words to go with the names of the animals.
4 Now put all the animals back in the bag and pass the bag round the circle, taking turns to choose an animal and saying 'I went to the zoo and I saw a...' If individual children find it difficult to think, work together to think of words to choose, but give them some thinking time and don't let the quick thinkers jump in too soon!

Key words and gestures

- Same
- Sound
- Animal
- Next

- Letter
- Listen
- Next
- Choose

Extending the challenge

- Play the same game but this time follow the rule of 'a bear in a box', 'a cat in a coat', a 'pig in a puddle' or a 'giraffe in a jumper'. You could provide the animals and the objects or items of clothing for the children to match.
- Use colours and animals such as 'a red reindeer' 'a brown bear' 'a yellow yak' or 'a blue beetle'.

TOP TIP
Tongue twisters are a good way of practising alliteration. Collect some simple ones and teach them to the children.

Involving parents

You could...
- *Help parents to understand the concept of alliteration by providing games, stories and poems to use at home.*
- *Make sure that parents know that listening is a difficult skill which needs enjoyable practice, not pressure!*

Look, listen and note

- *Some children catch the 'alliteration bug' very quickly and love making silly chants. This is a real talent, enjoy and recognise it!*
- *Note the children who still can't hear similarities in sounds and give them more activities where they can practice.*
- *Watch for enjoyment and involvement when you read alliterative poems and stories.*

Take it outside

- Play alliteration games outside...
- Using names: 'Come here smiling Sunita' 'Can you hear me careful Christopher?'
- Talking about objects you find in the garden: 'Look, a lovely leaf' 'I can hear a brilliant bird'
- Using alliteration when you go for walks: 'Let's walk on the green, green grass' 'Who can find a stunning stone or a pretty pebble?'
- Making alliterative rhymes and chants: 'Here we come with sticky, sticky sticks, walking on the path in the pretty park, scuffling in the scrunchy leaves and finding cones and conkers.'

Snack sounds

This core activity is suitable for a group of children.

What you need:

A range of fruits: apple slices, orange segments, pear, grapes, melon or pineapple cubes etc.

Raw vegetable sticks: carrot, celery, cucumber

Yoghurt dip

Kebab sticks

Plastic plates or bowls

Enhancing the activity

- Have some yogurt available for dipping the vegetable sticks, and say: 'Y-y-yogurt, d-d-dip. I will dip a carrot in the d-d-dip.'
- Add some more unusual fruit to extend the range of flavours.
- Make some snack tongue twisters and say them as fast as you can without getting mixed up: 'Red apple, yellow apple, red apple, yellow apple'
- Read together *Oliver's Fruit Salad* by Vivian French (Hodder Children's Books), *I Eat Fruit! And I Eat vegetables* by Hannah Tofts (Zero to Ten Publishers)

Snack time is a very good time for some language games and activities. This one focuses on initial sounds and alliteration and you can adapt it for the sort of snack you are offering or the children are preparing. We have used healthy snacks of fruit and vegetables.

What you do

1 Prepare the fruit and vegetables and put them on serving plates.
2 Sit in a circle with a plate each and the snack plates in the middle. Explain what you are going to do.
3 Say: 'This game is called Snack sounds and we are going to practise sounds as we snack'.
4 Now show the children what to do by taking some fruit as you say: 'I'll have some a-a-apple and some p-p-pear. I'll have some c-c-cucumber and then stop there'.
5 Now offer the snack plates to one of the children and help them to say the simple rhyme as they choose three different types of food.
6 When everyone has chosen their snack, enjoy eating together before offering more to any child who wants a second helping.

Look, listen and note

- *Some children find it very difficult to talk and move at the same time. These children will need to choose their fruit first and then talk about it.*
- *Watch for children who need more practice with initial sounds.*
- *Note the children who love these sorts of games, with a real sense of rhythm and fun. These children will enjoy poems and rhymes of all sorts.*

Key words and gestures

- Like
- Choose
- Say
- Rhyme
- Tongue twister
- Different
- Same
- Pattern
- Favourite

Extending the challenge

- Offer fruit slices and pieces and make patterns before you eat them, saying 'a-a-apple, p-p-pear, a-a-apple, g-g-grape, a-a-apple, r-r-r-raisin' as you point to each piece of fruit in the pattern.
- Make fruit kebabs in alternating patterns, saying this rhyme as you point to each part: 'Fruit kebab, fruit kebab, thread them on a stick. Apple, orange, apple, orange, grape, grape, grape'.

Take it outside

- Have snack time out of doors whenever you can – children love picnics!
- Play this game whenever you have a picnic or go on a visit. It will make lunch time a bit different.

TOP TIP
Make a tongue twister book for your book corner and add new ones when you think of them.

Involving parents

You could...
- *Suggest that parents could use the sounds of letters (not their letter names) when they are preparing food, asking children what they want or responding to what is for tea. 'I'm cooking something that starts with b.'*
- *Ask parents if they know any tongue twisters.*

Alphabet soup

This core activity is suitable for a group of children.

Enhancing the activity

- Use alphabet mats to help children learn the names, sounds and order of the letters of the alphabet. Add a basket of objects, so the children can place these on the initial sound of the objects' names.
- Find some more alphabet food items such as alphabet cereals, biscuits or sweets to expand the experience.
- Make your own alphabet posters or books: A Food Alphabet, An Alphabet of Names, An Alphabet of People. For ideas refer to *The Little Book of Games with Sounds* by Sally Featherstone (Featherstone A & C Black)
- Sing alphabet songs (Also in *The Little Book of Games with Sounds*)
- Share Abc3D by Marion Bataille (Roaring Brook Press) – a fascinating alphabet pop-up book for all ages, John Burningham's ABC (Jonathan Cape), *The Alphabet Book* (Dorling Kindersley).

Recognising the letters of the alphabet is a key skill in reading, and being familiar with the alphabet will give children a flying start in organising their knowledge of the letters and the sounds they make. Simple activities like this are easy to prepare and fun to do.

What you do

1. This activity is easier on a table, where the children can stand up to reach the letters they need.
2. Sit together and put the tray on a table in the middle.
3. Tip the pasta out of the bag and spread it out on the tray.
4. Let the children have time to touch, feel and play with the pasta before you start to do the activity.
5. Look at some of the letters, talking about capital letters and small letters. Most alphabet spaghetti and other alphabet foods are capital letters, but it's important for children to know about these as well as small or lower case letters.
6. Now see if the children can find the letter that starts their name. Get them to pick this letter up and put it on their plate. Some children may be able to find all the letters of their name.
7. Try with some other letters. Can the children find the letter that comes at the beginning of 'Cat' or Pig' – starting with words where the initial letter is the same shape in both lower and upper case. These are C, J, M, O, P, S, W and Z.
8. Let the children try making words using the tweezers to pick up the spaghetti letters.
9. Leave the letters out where the children can return to them in free play, reinforcing what they have learned during group time.

Extending the challenge

- Use other alphabet letters such as foam bath letters that stick on wet surfaces or magnetic letters that stick on baking trays or other metal surfaces.
- Find or buy some alphabet cutters for dough or salt pastry and make names or other words with them. Make these into permanent resources by baking them on a low heat to harden them and painting them with a mixture of paint and white glue. Add self-adhesive magnetic tape to turn them into magnetic letters.

Look, listen and note

- *Watch for children who find it difficult to learn the difference between letter names and their sounds. Give these children some extra practice in the ones they find difficult.*
- *Track the children's understanding of alphabet order.*
- *Observe and record children's developing ability to see the difference between capitals and lower case letters, particularly the difficult ones, such as G, T, A, D, E.*

Take it outside

- Mark alphabet stepping-stones or an alphabet snake on your path or patio. Use this for games, rhymes or alphabet challenges.
- Hang laminated card or plastic letters of the alphabet in bushes or on the fence and challenge the children to touch them in alphabet order.

TOP TIP
The door of an old freezer or fridge makes a great surface for magnetic letters.

Key words and gestures

- Alphabet
- Letters
- Sounds
- Names
- Look
- Listen
- Same
- Different
- Capital
- Name
- Word
- Beginning

Involving parents

You could...
- *Encourage parents to use lower case (small) letters as well as capitals when writing for their children, or teaching them how to write their names and other simple words. Explain the children need to know the lower case versions for learning to read.*

Put it on again

This activity is suitable for a small group of children.

What you need:

A large doll, teddy, empathy doll or your big 'Talking - Time' puppet (or two of these) – older children will enjoy working with more 'grown up' characters.

Some doll's clothes, baby clothes or smaller items of clothing that fit the characters

Some other objects such as a cup, a book, a hat, some glasses, a small basket, a small book, a pen, a purse with some money in it, a lollipop or a piece of fruit, a superhero toy, a comic, a blanket etc.

Involving parents

You could...
* Suggest to parents that using outgrown baby clothes to dress teddies and dolls gives children good practice for dressing themselves.
* Ask parents and others in the community if they know anyone who might make some doll's or teddy clothes for you!

This activity supports auditory memory and following instructions. It builds on 'Put it on' in Sounds Fun 30-50 months. If the children have not played the game before, make the instructions very simple at first, but maintain a sense of fun.

What you do

1 Sit together, look at all the objects and name each one.
2 Tell the children about the game you are going to play, explaining that you will ask each of them to work with the doll/teddy. If they have played the game before, remind them of the last time you played.
3 Now ask the first child to do something: 'Give the puppet a comic and a drink', 'Put a hat on the puppet's head' etc.
4 Make sure everyone gets a turn and ask each time whether the child has done what you asked. Give instructions that suit each child's ability and maturity, and praise them each time, helping them if necessary and involving the rest of the group in checking.
5 Return the clothing and other objects to the middle of the circle after each turn.
6 Now increase the challenge a bit by giving more complex instructions: 'Put the teddy under the chair with the cup and saucer'; 'Put a hat and a scarf on the puppet and put them inside the box'; 'Dress the teddy in some glasses, a hat and a pair of socks'. Help the child by reminding them of the instruction if necessary and let other children continue to support and check.
7 When each child has had a turn, decide whether to go on or not. If they have had enough, stop, and play the game again later.
8 If they are ready for more, you could ask them to do something different and unusual, such as 'Put a sock on the puppet's hand' or 'Put Superman on the dolls' head.'

Extending the challenge

* Ask children to do or make something simple for the character such as cut out a circle and put it on the character's head, fill a cup with water and put it by the teddy, fold a tissue twice and put it in the character's hand, put some money, a piece of paper for a list and a pen in the purse.
* Let the children work in pairs, one giving the instructions, the other following them. Let the rest of the group listen and check.
* When children are familiar with the game, you could make the instruction

Look, listen and note

- *Note which children can now follow more than one instruction, and who is ready to move on to more complex ones.*
- *Watch for children who are beginning to be able to follow a more complex series of instructions and continue to increase the challenge for these children. Other children who are not yet so advanced will benefit from watching them. These children will be getting a much deeper experience through watching.*

Take it outside

- If you have an empathy doll, get some extra clothes from a catalogue so you can play this game outside, dressing it in sports kit or character costumes.
- Incorporate your outdoor equipment in the game by working on positional words such as: 'at the top of the climbing frame', 'behind the shed', 'under the slide', 'between the bushes and the fence'.

Enhancing the activity

- Add more objects, such as a pair of scissors, some paper, some small squares of fabric, some tissues, a necklace or a watch.
- Read *The Emperor's New Clothes* by Mike Gordon (Usborne) or *Pants and More Pants* by Giles Andreae and Nick Sharratt (Corgi).
- Adapt the rhyme *Here we go round the Mulberry bush* to a dressing rhyme: *Here are the clothes for Superman, Superman, Superman... This is the way we put on his cloak, put on his cloak, put on his cloak ... etc.*

TOP TIP
Look in charity shops for second hand baby clothes.

Key words and gestures

- Funny
- Silly
- Dress
- Arms
- Legs
- Feet

- Head
- Clothes
- Unusual
- Instruction
- Together

Chinese whispers

This activity is suitable for a small group of children.

What you need:

A quiet place for listening

Your 'Talking - Time' puppet or another character (optional)

Enhancing the activity

- It sometimes helps to pass a small object such as a shell round as the whisper passes from child to child. This does help with concentration and turn-taking, as long as the object is familiar, otherwise it can just be a distraction.
- Try standing up to whisper, still in a circle.
Adapt the rhyme *'I hear thunder'* to a whispering rhyme:
Can you whisper?
Can you whisper?
I can too, I can too,
Whisper round the circle, whisper round the circle,
Pass it on, pass it on.

'Chinese whispers' is an old party game. We have updated it here to give children practice in listening carefully to each other and moderating their voices. You can use a puppet or soft toy to start the game and model the whispering.

What you do

1 Sit together in a circle, close enough to whisper. Introduce the puppet or character and explain that they will be helping with the game.
2 Explain tat the puppet will whisper something to you and you will whisper it to the child next to you. They will pass it along in a whisper until it has gone right round the circle, back to you again. Then you will say what the last child said to you. The aim of the game is to get the word, or phrase all the way round the circle without a change.
3 Have a practice round. Whisper your name to the child next to you and pass this round the circle. When your name gets back to you, check whether it has changed through the whispering.
4 Now play again. This time, try a short phrase such as 'It's raining outside', 'It's Tuesday tomorrow' or 'Sophie's got a red shirt on'.
5 See how well the children convey the message by listening carefully and passing it on accurately. If the message is garbled or changed by the time it returns to you, don't make the children feel responsible, just laugh and make it fun!
6 If the children can pass a simple message successfully, make it a bit more challenging by sending a nonsense message such as 'Wiggly worms', 'Six sizzling sausages' or 'Put a penny in your pocket'.

Take it outside

- Whispering games out of doors are much harder, as there is always background noise. However, they are very good practice for older children! Try giving instructions, choosing groups or sending simple messages by whispering.
- Have some quiet times outside where children are encouraged to listen for small sounds in the environment such as distant planes and traffic, leaves rustling, small birds singing, tyres on the paving, a ball bouncing, raindrops or falling leaves.

TOP TIP
Hunt the thimble' (or another small object) is good for practising loud and soft voices.

Look, listen and note

- *Watch for children who consistently mis-hear during this game. They may need a hearing test.*
- *Children's hearing sometimes varies according to the seasons, with hearing improving in the Spring and decreasing in the Winter months. Be aware of this as you observe children's responses.*
- *Note the children who are very good at hearing low sounds and small noises. Make sure you give these children praise and recognition for this very important skill.*

Extending the challenge

- Stand in a line to whisper and the last child in the line runs back to you for the final whisper.
- Have a basket of objects in the middle of the circle and whisper instructions to individual children: 'Take the brick to Caroline', 'Put the hat on Charlie's head' or 'Wrap the superhero in the scarf and give it to Kishan'.
- Send a message part way round the group. Tell the children that the message or instruction is for one of them. Start the whispered message off, and when it gets to the right child, they must do what it says.

Involving parents

You could...
- *Make sure parents know how important hearing is to talking, reading and learning. Encourage them to talk to their doctor or practice nurse if they have worries about their child's hearing.*
- *Colds and other infections often affect children 's hearing. Keep in touch with the parents of children who are susceptible to ear infections or glue ear.*

Key words and gestures

- Whisper
- Listen
- Pass it on
- Careful
- Difficult
- Neighbour
- Circle
- Line
- Puppet
- First/last
- Together

Make a name

This activity is suitable for a small group of children.

Recognising initial letter sounds is a vital skill and needs plenty of practice. This game uses children's names and their photos to encourage recognition of letters and the details of faces.

What you do

1 Sit together in a circle, and look at both sets of cards. Let each child find their own initial letter card and their photo. Talk about the capital letters at the beginning of everyone's names, and make sure all the children in the group can recognise them.
2 Put the letter cards in one bag and the photos in the other bag.
3 Use the letter cards bag first.
4 Offer the bag to one child and let them pick a card. They look at the letter, say the sound, then look round the circle, saying the sound till they find the right child to give it to: P-P-P-Paul.
5 This child checks the letter card and if it's right, they choose the next card from the bag.
6 Continue until all the children have had a turn.
7 Now take the other bag and let one child choose a photo card. They look at the card and say something about the child in the photo: 'This is Sam, she's got blue eyes/curly hair/pink cheeks etc'. Then they give the card to the right child.

Enhancing the activity

- Add the photos and initial letter cards of the adults in your setting.
- Play the same game with animals and initial letter cards. Each child chooses an animal and the letter cards go in a bag.
- Read *My Name Is Not Isabella* by Jennifer Fosberry (Monkey Barrel Press), *I'm Special* by Paul Humphrey (Zero to Ten)
- Adapt the rhyme Frere Jacques' to a name song:
  What is my name, what is my name, Can you guess, can you guess? Look at my name letter, look at my name letter,

Extending the challenge

- Use photos of the children taken from the back or of just their eyes or part of their face – this is much harder.
- Make the letters from adhesive sandpaper or felt so the child can feel the letter in the bag and say the sound before they take the card out.

TOP TIP
Simple sound games like 'I'm thinking of something that starts with the m sound are very helpful'.

Involving parents

You could...
- *Encourage parents to play initial sound games with their children.*
- *Make sure parents know how important hearing is to talking, reading and learning. Encourage them to talk to their doctor or practice nurse if they have worries about their child's hearing.*

Look, listen and note

- *Watch for children who find it really difficult to link a sound to a name. They will need support and more practice.*
- *Be aware that some children have hearing problems in the winter due to glue ear.*
- *Note the children who are very good at hearing these sounds and seeing small differences in photos. Make sure you give these children praise and recognition for this very important skill.*

Key words and gestures

- Guess
- Look
- Different
- Who
- Right

- Sound
- Look
- Eyes
- Hair
- Colour

Take it outside

- Any sound game can be played out of doors. How abut drawing some chalk circles so the children can group themselves by letter name, hair colour, eye colour, etc?
- Offer chalk or water and brushes so children can practise writing, mark making and drawing out of doors on walls and paths.

What's moved?

This core activity is suitable for a group of children.

What you need:

A small world set: a train layout, airport, roadway, farm, town or park

Cars, people, animals and other moveable objects

A camera (optional)

A screen or curtain (fabric pegged on a washing line so you can hide the scene)

Enhancing the activity

- Play the game with a scene in a sand or water tray.
- Use story characters, superhero figures or make an underwater scene.
- Share *Spot the Difference* books such as *Spot the Differences* by Steven Rosen (Scholastic), *Spot the Difference: Animals* by Rebecca Rissman (Heinemann), *Ears* by Daniel Nunn (Heinemann).
- Adapt 'The wheels on the bus' to a changes song:
  The things on the farm are moving round, moving round,

This game is about reasoning and about spotting small differences in position and place. If the children help with setting up the scene, this will help them to get involved. 'Spot the difference' books and comics are very good practice for reading, as they train the eye and the brain to look for differences in letters and words.

What you do

1. Work with the children to set up a scene. You will need to decide how complex to make it in order to fit the age and maturity of the group.
2. When the scene is complete, let the children play with it for a while. Then ask them to look very carefully to see where everything is because you are going to move something and see if they can spot it.
3. You could take a photo at this stage if you like, so the children can check the original if they can't spot what has changed.
4. Now hide the scene behind the curtain or other screen, and move one thing. At first you should make this a fairly obvious move and a larger piece.
5. Draw back the screen and see if the children can spot what has changed.
6. Help them to put the change into words e.g. 'The yellow car was by the house, now it's in front of the church.'
7. Continue to play as a group, moving one thing at a time and either asking the whole group or individuals to spot the difference.
8. When children are used to the game, a child could be the mover.

Key words and gestures

- Same
- Different
- Place
- Moved
- Think
- Look
- Carefully
- Remember
- Brain
- Eyes

Extending the challenge

- Move two things at a time.
- Turn the tray or mat round to make it even more different.

TOP TIP
Take some photos of familiar objects for 'Spot the difference' games.

Look, listen and note

- Note the children who find this game really difficult and give them some practice in a simpler layout.
- Spotting differences is a real strength of some children and this will help them with reading.
- Seeing differences in pictures is very good practice — make sure you observe how well individual children can do this.

Take it outside

- Try moving equipment or objects in your outdoor area and see if the children can spot the difference.
- Put an inside object outside and see if children can spot it when they go out.
- Play 'Spot who moved' as a group. One child looks at where children are standing like statues, then turns their back on the group. One of the children moves — can the chosen child spot the child who has moved?

Involving parents

You could...

- Encourage parents to join their children in playing 'Spot the difference' games in comics and books.
- Families could play this game at home using kitchen implements, toys or even cans and boxes from the food cupboard.
- Encourage parents to join their children in playing 'Spot the difference' games in comics and books.
- Families could play this game at home using kitchen implements, toys or even cans and boxes from the food cupboard.

Two word game

This core activity is suitable for a group of children.

What you need:

Enough familiar objects from your setting for one for each child: a Lego brick, a toy car, a mug, a small world character, a large bead, a sock, a glove, a hat, a shoe etc.

A cloth bag, big enough to hold all the objects – a pillowcase would do nicely!

Enhancing the activity

- Play the game with small world animals or characters.
- Collect some fabric samples of different textures to make a 'feely describing bag'.
- Try The Little Book of Colour, Shape and Number by Clare Beswick (Featherstone Education/A & C Black)
- Share *Mr Rabbit and the Lovely Present* by Charlotte Zolotow (HarperCollins) or *The Little Mouse, the Red Ripe Strawberry, and the Big Hungry Bear* by Audrey Wood (Child's Play).

This game helps children with descriptive words. Single 'name' words or nouns are the first words children use, so the next stage is to provide practice in adding adjectives to describe objects that they know.

What you do

1 Sit together and look at all the objects you have collected. Make sure the children know the name of each one. As the children name the objects ask them if they can say anything else about it – its colour, size, the way it feels, its shape etc. because you are going to play the 'Two word game'.
2 Put all the objects in the bag.
3 Now pass the bag to one of the children and let them take out one object.
4 Ask them if they can say two things about the object – its' name and something else about it such as a big brick, a red car, a shiny cup, a heavy boot, a warm glove. Help them if they need it.
5 Now pass the bag on for the next child to choose an object.
6 Remember to give plenty of praise for thinking of and saying describing words. Don't worry if children copy each other and say the same word, as long as they are thinking.
7 Continue until everyone has had a turn.
8 Now put the objects back in the bag, echoing their words: 'In goes a red glove, in goes a blue car, in goes a shiny button, in goes a square bead, in goes a lumpy Lego brick' etc.

Extending the challenge

- Try thinking of three words about the object.
- Encourage children to think of other words rather than just simple colours. This is much more difficult.

TOP TIP
Boys generally need more time to learn colour and texture words than girls do.

Look, listen and note

- *Some children find this step difficult, be patient and keep on modelling the language you want.*
- *If you notice that some children can think of descriptive words more easily, praise their efforts and raise your expectations.*
- *Remember that children who are learning English may be slower in gaining this more elaborate language.*
- *Note examples of descriptive language that individual children use*

Key words and gestures

- Words
- Colours
- Shapes
- Look
- Feel
- Another
- Choose
- Inside
- Size
- More
- Describe

Take it outside

- When you are out of doors, get into the habit of using additional descriptive words as you talk, play and enjoy the garden. Talk about the big blue sky, the fluffy white clouds, the soft green grass, the drippy wet leaves.
- Try just sitting or lying down with some of the children and talking about what you can see and hear.

Involving parents

You could...
- *Encourage parents to use two word descriptions when they talk to their children.*
- *Colour names and textures are good types of words to use. Help parents by providing some books with descriptive texts.*

Find a letter

This core activity is suitable for a small group of children.

What you need:

Sand, flour, compost or paper shreddings

Plastic or card letters (lower case)

Small objects with initial sounds to match the letters

Enhancing the activity

- Hide the initial letters of all the children's names. They must hunt for their own letter.
- Hide initial letters of names or objects and initial letters around the room and have a letter hunt.
- Read *The Treasure Hunt* by Nick Butterworth (Picture Lions), *Maisy's Pirate Treasure Hunt* by Lucy Cousins (Candlewick Press) or *Spot's Treasure Hunt* by Eric Hill (Puffin).

Looking for hidden treasure is a great experience. This game combines treasure hunting and letter recognition. Sand and other tactile materials are ideal and are favourite activities of most children.

What you do

1 Sit together and look at all the objects you have collected and the matching letters. Make sure all the children know the names and letter sounds and can recognise the written forms.
2 Tell the children about the 'Treasure Hunt' and that you are going to hide the objects and letters in the sand.
3 Hide the letters and objects.
4 Now the children take turns to find a matching letter and object.
5 They must say the letter sound and the object name, then hide them again.

TOP TIP
Try setting the letters in jelly!

Look, listen and note

- *Note the children who can maintain their concentration when looking for particular objects or letters.*
- *Look for children who find the task difficult and perhaps arrange for a smaller version in a washing up bowl.*
- *Take account of children who are learning English and make sure they are confident with the sounds and objects. Reduce the number if necessary.*

Key words and gestures

- Letters
- Sounds
- Find
- Match
- Pair
- Name
- Hunt
- Treasure
- Search
- Under
- Hidden

Extending the challenge

- Hide letters round the room. Give each child an object and let them hunt for the letter card or give the child the letter card and they must find the hidden object.
- Hide a quantity of objects in sand or around the room. Children collect the objects and place them on an alphabet mat, matching the objects to the letters.

Take it outside

- Organise treasure hunts out of doors where there are lots of hiding places for objects and letters.
- If you have an outdoor sand pit you could have a really big 'Treasure Hunt' with spades and even pirate costumes!

Involving parents

You could...
- *Encourage parents to play these games with bath letters and bubbles or magnetic letters on a baking tray of flour.*
- *Suggest going on 'Treasure Hunt' walks in the park to collect natural treasures to bring to your setting.*

Mystery object

This core activity is suitable for a group of children.

What you need:

A fabric bag with an elastic or ribbon drawstring

A few unusual objects such as a pineapple, a massage roller, a Christmas decoration, a jelly mould, a lemon squeezer, a garlic press, a coconut, a shoe horn and a potato masher

Enhancing the activity

- Offer the bag and some objects for free play.
- Make a display of unusual objects.
- Read *Little Grey and the Great Mystery* by Rachel Rivett (Lion Hudson), *The Great Pie Robbery and Other Mysteries* by Richard Scarry (Sterling) or *Puzzle Ocean* by Susannah Leigh (Usborne).

'Feely bags' are familiar to most early years practitioners. In this game, children will be experiencing, describing and talking about objects they can only feel, and may have never seen before. Some children will find this really hard, so don't make the game too long.

What you do

1 The first time you play this game, concentrate on only one object. It's better to spend some time on one thing than try to cram too much in, or go on too long.
2 Put an object in the bag before you gather the children together.
3 Tell the children that you have a mystery object in the bag and you want to see if they can talk about what it might be, without seeing it.
4 Go round the group and offer the bag to each child so they can put their hand in the top. Keep hold of the bag yourself. Remember, some children may not like putting their hand in a bag if they can't see what is in it. Let these children watch until they feel more confident.
5 Now ask each child if they can say one thing about the mystery object. Give them some help if they need it. Ask questions such as 'What does it feel like?' 'What do you think it is made from?' 'Is it smooth or lumpy?' 'Is it warm?'
6 Accept all their suggestions. Give them plenty of thinking time and another feel if they want it.
7 When you have collected all the ideas, ask if anyone knows what the object is.
8 Now invite one of the children to take the object out of the bag and look at it together, passing it round the group. What do the children think now?
9 Show them how the object works and what it is for.
10 Don't go on too long – one object is probably enough for children of this age.

Take it outside

- Leave mystery objects in your outdoor area for children to find.
- Look for puzzling things such as strange shaped leaves or clouds.

Look, listen and note

- *Some children love mysteries and challenges, others hate them and find them very threatening. Watch the children.*
- *Note those children who are making guesses and thinking up descriptions for themselves. These children are ready for all sorts of challenges and exciting things to think about.*
- *Take account of children who are learning English. They may find this sort of activity more challenging than some more fluent members of the group.*

Key words and gestures

- Think
- Feel
- Careful
- Might
- Guess

- Mystery
- Puzzle
- Words
- Describe
- Touch

Extending the challenge

- Collect a bag of unusual objects and use them for story telling. Start a made-up story and when you need a new idea, let a child take an object out of the bag and tell you what it is and what happens next.
- Collect some pictures (Google Images has great photos and pictures) or take photos of unusual angles or close-ups of everyday things. Use these for discussions and games, or make a 'Mystery Book'.

TOP TIP
Look in charity shops for unusual items to add to your mystery object collection.

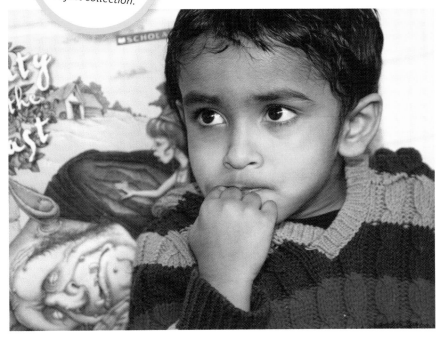

Involving parents

You could...
- *Encourage parents to have fun with their children – games and challenges are good fun for families.*
- *Grandparents may have some mystery objects to intrigue their grandchildren and turn into a game for all three generations.*

'Each Peach Pear Plum'

This core activity is suitable for a small group of children.

What you need:

A book with rhyming text – we have used 'Each Peach, Pear, Plum' by Janet and Allan Ahlberg but you could adapt the activity for any rhyming text you have in your collection.

Enhancing the activity

- Make a story bag for the book, with clues for each page.
- Stick an envelope in the back cover of the book, and hide some small sheets with the words to all the stories and rhymes in the book.
- Some more rhyming stories for your collection might include *The Gruffalo* and other books by Julia Donaldson (Macmillan), *Don't Put Your Finger in the Jelly, Nellie* and *Elephant Wellyphant* and lots of other rhyming titles, by Nick Sharrat (Scholastic), *Pass the Jam, Jim* and *Need a Trim Jim?* By Kaye Umanski (Red Fox), *This is the Bear* and *This is the Bear in the Scary Night* by

There are lots of storybooks with rhyming text and it's a good idea to look out for these and remember where they are. Children love rhyming text. Some of the best-loved stories have rhyming text and a real sense of rhythm. These stories really help children to develop an experience and knowledge of rhyme and rhythm, and are an enjoyable way to start a shared activity.

What you do

1 Make sure the group is small enough for all the children to see the detail in the pictures. This story is about visual clues as well as auditory or listening ones.
2 Read the book right through, just pausing long enough on each page for the children to see the next character or characters hiding in the picture.
3 Now return to the start and read the story again. This time, pause before the name of the next characters and wait for the children to finish the sentence. Praise their efforts in completing the rhyme and finding the clues.
4 If the children are ready for more, say or sing some of the nursery rhymes in the book.

Extending the challenge

- Collect some more rhyming stories to use in these sessions. Let children choose which one to share and leave these where they can read them in freeplaysessions.
- Make your own rhyming book, either a version of one in your collection or a new story with your own rhymes.

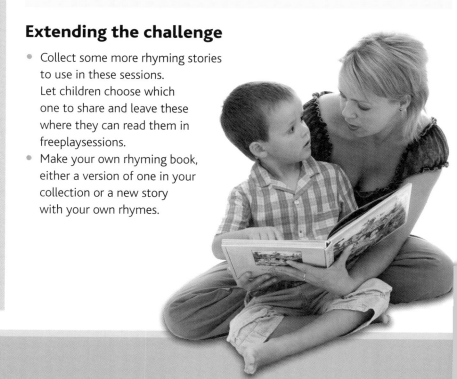

Look, listen and note

- *Watch for children who love silly rhymes and rhythmical sounds. Ask these children to demonstrate their enjoyment for others and teach their friends how to do it.*
- *Let children take a turn at telling the story. This will give you time to observe their development and watch the responses of the others in the group.*
- *Watch for those children who always respond slightly later than others. This often reveals a lack of confidence in the activity.*

Key words and gestures

- Rhyme
- Listen
- Word
- Story
- Next

- Wonder
- Guess
- Hiding
- Surprise
- Ending

TOP TIP
'Playful' adults make a big contribution to children's learning!

Take it outside

- Use rhymes and rhyming songs when you play outside. Nonsense rhymes are just as much fun as those that make sense.
- Encourage children to vocalise in rhyme as they run, ride, play and climb, making rhymes such as 'jump, tump, pump, lump, crump'; 'down, sown, town, mown, frown' and 'hop, hop, pop, pop, stop, stop'. Play these sound games with them.

Involving parents

You could...
- *Make some books, rhyme sheets or CDs available for parents to borrow, and encourage them to share the rhymes they know with their children. Nursery rhymes are vital for early readers.*
- *Encourage parents to sing along to radio, CD and TV with their children. Any sort of singing helps both rhythm and rhyme.*

Story sack: 'The Gruffalo'

This core activity is suitable for a group of children.

What you need:

The Gruffalo by Julia Donaldson (Macmillan)

A fabric bag, big enough for all the things you will collect! Some practitioners use child-sized backpacks, carrier bags, shoes bags or gift bags with relevant pictures or designs on them.

For this story, you could have finger puppets of a mouse, a fox, an owl, a snake and a Gruffalo. (You could make a Gruffalo glove puppet from a brown sock or a mitten and stick eyes with poisonous wart, horns, teeth, and feet). You could add some trees, butterflies or anything else from the story, so more children can join in the retelling.

Story sacks are an easy way to bring books to life. Children love to have objects to handle, and using all their senses will increase their enjoyment and understanding of the story. Make some story sacks for your favourite books, or borrow some from a library loan or Literacy collection.

What you do

1 Sit together in a group, making sure all the children can see the book.
2 Read the book once, right through, encouraging the children to join in if they know the story.
3 Now show the children the contents of your story sack. Take the objects out one at a time and pass them round so every child can see and touch them. Talk about the Gruffalo and his special features.
4 Ask the children who would like to help to tell the story again, this time with the characters. Choose one child for each character and remind them to hold their puppet up at the right time in the story.
5 Now read the story together, encouraging the children to bring each puppet in at the right point in the story and emphasising the rhyme and rhythm of the words.
6 Leave the story sack where children can play the story again in their own freeplay sessions.

Extending the challenge

- Make your own version of the Gruffalo, where the mouse meets some more animals.
- Start playing 'onset and rime' games (separating the rhyme bit from the rest of the word). Use these to explore strings of rhyming words e.g. bat/hat/cat/rat/sat or fr-og, d-og, l-og. Rhyming is now seen as a key skill in becoming a confident reader.

TOP TIP
Try to include items to stimulate all the senses – smell and texture are important for learning.

Key words and gestures

• Rhyme	• Different
• Listen	• Word
• Sound	• Story
• Same	• Ending

Look, listen and note

- *Rhyming is a skill. Some children will be able to follow a rhyme, or even finish a rhyming sentence, but not make up their own rhymes. Be patient, but remember it is a very important skill.*
- *Some children will love rhymes, rhyming texts and rhyming stories, and will make up their own rhymes and songs.*
- *Children who are learning English may well be able to rhyme in their first or home language, but not in English. Make sure you listen carefully to their speech and note their emerging ability even if this needs translating.*

Enhancing the activity

- Make some more story sacks of favourite stories, particularly those with good rhythm and rhyming text.
- Collect some pairs of rhyming objects to use in matching games and for making up simple rhyming stories such as a boat and a coat, a bag and a flag, a hat and a cat, a bear and a pear, a snake and a cake, a tree and a bee, a spoon and a moon, a sock and a rock etc.
- Share more rhyming texts from Julia Donaldson: *The Gruffalo's Child, Room on the Broom, A Squash and a Squeeze* and *The Snail and the Whale* (all published by Macmillan).

Take it outside

- Play out rhyming stories out of doors by offering props and simple items such as masks, ears and tails.
- Make a simple stage area for role-playing stories, karaoke, concerts and other performances that children invent themselves.

Involving parents

You could...
- *Encourage parents who speak more than one language to contribute songs, rhymes and stories from other languages.*
- *Keep encouraging singing, nursery rhymes and other games with words. Offer some ideas for these in a take-home booklet.*

Books list

An expanded compilation of books and stories for supporting early phonics. This list has been compiled to help you in your work with Letters and Sounds in reception classes, and includes all the books suggested on the activity pages.

Books of activities for speaking and listening
- L is for Sheep – Getting ready for phonics, Ed Sally Featherstone (Featherstone/A&C Black)
- The Little Book of Colour, Shape and Number, Clare Beswick; (Featherstone Education/A & C Black)
- The Little Book of Games with Sounds, Sally Featherstone (Featherstone/A & C Black)
- The Little Book of Listening, Clare Beswick (Featherstone Education/A & C Black)

Stories
- Brown Bear, Brown Bear, What Do You See?; Eric Carle (Puffin Books)
- Froggy Plays in the Band, Jonathan London (Puffin Books)
- Goldilocks and the Three Bears, John Kurtz (Jump at the Sun)
- Little Beaver and the Echo, Amy MacDonald (Walker Books)
- Little Grey and the Great Mystery, Rachel Rivett (Lion Hudson)
- Maisy's Pirate Treasure Hunt, Lucy Cousins (Candlewick Press)
- My Name Is Not Isabella, Jennifer Fosberry (Monkey Barrel Press)
- Mr Rabbit and the Lovely Present, Charlotte Zolotow; (HarperCollins)
- Noah's Ark and the Christmas Story (Say the Sounds), Victoria Tebbs (Usborne Books)
- Noisy Fairy Tales (Ladybird Books)
- Noisy Town, Noisy Jungle, Noisy Zoo, Noisy Animals, Noisy Dinosaurs (all from Usborne Books)
- Oliver's Fruit Salad, Vivian French (Hodder Children's Books)
- Pants, and More Pants, Giles Andreae (Corgi)
- Phonic Stories for Young Readers, a series of six titles, Phil Roxbee Cox (Usborne Books)
- Richard Scarry's The Great Pie Robbery and Other Mysteries, Richard Scarry (Sterling)
- Rosie's Walk, Pat Hutchins, (Bodley Head)
- Spot's Treasure Hunt, Eric Hill (Puffin)
- The Emperor's New Clothes, Mike Gordon (Usborne)
- The Happy Hedgehog Band, Martin Waddell (Walker Books)
- The Little Mouse, the Red Ripe Strawberry, and the Big Hungry Bear, Audrey Wood (Child's Play)
- The Listening Walk, Paul Showers (HarperCollins)

- The Listening Walk, David Kirk (Grosset and Dunlap)
- The Treasure Hunt, Nick Butterworth (Picture Lions)

Rhyming stories
- A Squash and a Squeeze, Julia Donaldson (Macmillan)
- Bumpus, Jumpus, Dinosaurumpus, Tony Mitton (Orchard Book)
- Don't Put Your Finger in the Jelly, Nellie, Nick Sharratt (Scholas
- Down by the Cool of the Pool, Tony Mitton (Orchard Books)
- Elephant Wellyphant, Nick Sharratt (Scholastic)
- Pass the Jam, Jim and Need a Trim Jim? Kaye Umanski (Red Fc
- Room on a Broom, Julia Donaldson (Macmillan)
- The Gruffalo, Julia Donaldson (Macmillan)
- The Gruffalo's Child, Julia Donaldson (Macmillan)
- The Snail and the Whale, Julia Donaldson (Macmillan)
- This is the Bear, Sarah Hayes (Walker Books)
- This is the Bear in the Scary Night, Sarah Hayes (Walker Book.
- Stomp, Chmp, Big jaws, Here Come the Dinosaurs, Kaye Umar (Puffin)
- Tabby McTat, Julia Donaldson (Macmillan)

Some alphabet books
- ABC, Brian Wildsmith (Star Bright Books)
- Abc3D, by Marion Bataille (Roaring Brook Press)
- John Burningham's ABC (Jonathan Cape)
- Picture This, Alison Jay (Templar)
- The Alphabet Book (Dorling Kindersley)
- The Dinosaur Alphabet Book, Jerry Pallotta (Charlesbridge)

Some audio stories
- Goldilocks and the Three Bears, Three Pigs, and Red Riding Hood and other traditional tales, Estelle Corke (Child's Play International)
- Harry and the Bucketful of Dinosaurs Book and CD (Puffin)
- Hairy McLary story collection, Lynley Dodd (Puffin)
- Jack and The Beanstalk and other Stories (BBC Children's Audi
- Three Little Pigs and other Stories (BBC Children's Audio)

Poetry and rhymes

- My Book of Rhyming Words & Phrase, Shinobu Akaishi; (Kumon Publishing)
- Noisy Poems, Jill Bennett (OUP)
- Tasty Poems by Jill Bennett (OUP)
- Tongue Twisters to Tangle Your Tongue, Rebecca Cobb (Marion Boyars Publishing)
- Twinkle Twinkle Chocolate Bar, John Foster (OUP)
- What's on the Menu? Bobbye S. Goldstein (Puffin Books)

Non fiction books

- Ears, Daniel Nunn (Heinemann)
- I Eat Fruit! And I Eat vegetables, Hannah Tofts (Zero to Ten)
- I'm Special, Paul Humphrey (Zero to Ten)
- Listen, Listen, Phillis Gershator (Barefoot Books)
- Noisy Worlds – Jungle, Zoo, Ocean, Night Time, Maurice Pledger (Templar)
- Oxford First Rhyming Dictionary, John Foster (OUP)
- Puzzle Ocean, Susannah Leigh (Usborne)
- Spot the Differences, Steven Rosen (Scholastic)
- Spot the Difference: Animals, Rebecca Rissman (Heinemann)
- Sweet as a Strawberry! And Cool as a Cucumber, Sally Smallwood (Zero to Ten)
- What's Hiding in There? Daniela Drescher (Floris Books)
- Where's Wally? Martin Handford (Walker Books)
- Who's Hiding on the Farm, Fiona Watt (Usborne)
- Who's Hiding at Home? Julie Fletcher (Campbell Books)
- Whole World, Christopher Corr (Barefoot Books)

Books about starting school

- Maisy Goes to Playschool, Lucy Cousins (Walker Books)
- My First Day at Nursery School, Becky Edwards (Bloomsbury)
- Start School (Topsy & Tim), Jean Adamson (Ladybird)
- Starting School, Allan and Janet Ahlberg (Puffin)

Books about sounds

- Boom Boom, Beep Beep, Roar! David Diehl (Stirling)
- First Picture Trucks, Building Site, Town: with sounds, Felicity Brooks (Usborne)
- Making Sounds, Charlotte Guillain (Heinemann)

Rhyming, rhythm, clapping and beat

- Beat Baby and Beat Baby rhymes and raps www.educationalpublications.com

- Bobby Shaftoe Clap Your Hands, Sue Nicholls (A & C Black)
- Clapping Games: Whole Brain Workouts for Lively Children, Jenny Mosley (Positive Press)
- Mr Tig Tog, Ros Bayley and Lynn Broadbent (Lawrence Educational Books)
- The Book of Call and Response: You Sing, John M. Feierabend (GIA Publications)
- The Book of Tapping and Clapping, John M. Feierabend (GIA Publications)

Music, action songs and nursery rhymes

- 101 Rhythm Instrument Activities: For Young Children, Abigail Flesch Connors (Gryphon House)
- Bingo Lingo: Supporting Literacy with Songs and Rhymes, Helen MacGregor (A & C Black)
- Bobby Shaftoe Clap Your Hands, by Sue Nicholls (A & C Black)
- Head, Shoulders, Knees and Toes: Clap, Wriggle, Stretch and Jump, Brian Moses (Franklin Watts)
- Kids Make Music: Clapping and Tapping from Bach to Rock; Avery Hart (Williamson)
- Let's Go, Zudie-o, Helen MacGregor (A & C Black)
- Make Music! Julia Lawson (Evans Brothers)
- Okki-Tokki-Unga: Action Songs for Children, Beatrice Harrop (A & C Black)
- The Handy Band, Sue Nicholls (A&C Black)
- The I Can't Sing Book: For Grownups Who Can't Carry a Tune But Want to Do Music with Young Children, Jackie Silberg (Brilliant Publications)
- Three Tapping Teddies: Musical Stories and Chants for the Very Young, Kaye Umansky (A & C Black)
- Toddler Play, Dr Wendy S Masi (Creative Publishing International)
- Music Express Foundation Stage, Sue Nicholls (A & C Black)
- Oranges and Lemons: Singing and Dancing Games, Karen King (OUP)
- This Little Puffin: the classic collection of Nursery Rhymes, Elizabeth Matterson (Puffin Books)

Making musical instruments

- Pat a Cake, Make and Shake: Make and Play Your Own Musical Instruments, Sue Nicholls (A&C Black)
- The Little Book of Junk Music: Little Books with Big Ideas, Simon Macdonald (A & C Black/Featherstone)

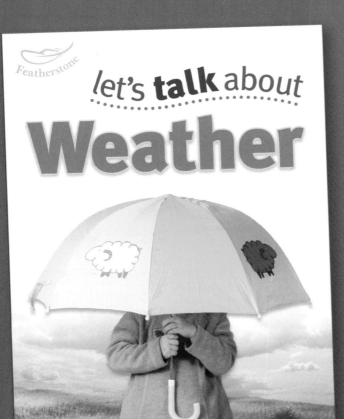

let's **talk** about

Weather

ISBN 978-1-4081-2668-4

let's **talk** about
Toys

ISBN 978-1-4081-2667-7

let's **talk** about
the Park

ISBN 978-1-4081-2669-1

let's **talk** about
Farms

ISBN 978-1-4081-2666-0

This exciting new series covers the six EYFS areas of learning and development through a variety of age appropriate themes. It fulfils the aims of the Every Child a Talker initiative.

Let's talk about... provides practitioners and children with entertaining, exciting and stimulating language activities that foster and enhance early language learning.

lly Featherstone and Su Wall

Sounds
Fun

40–60+
months

Published 2010 by A&C Black Publishers Limited
36 Soho Square, London, W1D 3QY
www.acblack.com

ISBN 978-1-4081-1465-0

Copyright © A&C Black Publishers Ltd 2010

Written by Sally Featherstone and Su Wall
Design by Trudi Webb
Photographs © Shutterstock, Fotolia and Rebecca Skerne

With thanks to the following schools for their help with the photos:
Valley Children's Centre (Rotherham) and Yarm Preparatory School (Stockton-on-Tees)

Printed in Great Britain by Latimer Trend & Company Limited

A CIP record for this publication is available from the British Library.

To see our full range of titles
Visit www.acblack.com/featherstone

Contents

Introduction 4

In the bag 8

Walks outside 10

Teddy's lost 12

Ears hear 14

I went to the shops 16

Echo me 18

Tell me where 20

Mystery sounds 22

Special names 24

I say, you say 26

Our kazoo band 28

Body sound patterns 30

Tap that name 32

Karaoke 34

Tape recorder fun 36

Follow the pattern 38

Make and shake 40

Find a rhyming friend 42

Repetitive rhymes 44

Goldilocks 46

Ring games 48

Jelly on a plate 50

On the washing line 52

I went to the zoo… 54

Snack sounds 56

Alphabet soup 58

Put it on again 60

Chinese whispers 62

Make a name 64

What's moved? 66

Two word game 68

Find a letter 70

Mystery object 72

'Each Peach Pear Plum' 74

Story sack: 'The Gruffalo' 76

Book list 78

Introduction

The best environment for communication

It is now well known that communication skills such as eye contact, body language, listening and speaking are at the heart of all learning and development. Children with good communication skills grow up to be confident members of society, who can use their skills to make the most of life inside and out of the education system. We also know that babies and children who, for various reasons, do not develop these skills in early childhood are at risk throughout the rest of their lives. They may fail to make strong relationships with others, they may be less successful in their working lives, and find learning much more difficult.

Such knowledge about language development has resulted in government initiatives such as *Every Child a Talker, Communication Matters* and *Letters and Sounds*, which are intended to support practitioners as they work with babies and children in the ever-increasing range of childcare provision. Some babies and children now spend more time in day care than they do at home, so the role of practitioners in supporting language development is very important, not just for those children growing up in disadvantaged or lone parent families, but those where both parents work long hours, where the home language is not English, or where the many other pressures of modern life mean that families spend less time together.

While the environment for communication in the early years should ideally replicate the best home situation, there are some factors which practitioners in settings may need to take into account when evaluating their own settings. The impact of radio, television, computers, mobile phones and constant background music has had a significant effect on children's ability to listen, speak and concentrate.

- Practitioners should be aware of these features of home life and restrict the use of television and computers in their setting as much as possible. In fact, many experts say that babies and children should have little or no television or computer exposure until they are three years old. This ideal is perhaps unrealistic in children's home lives, but we should make every effort to counteract this in early years settings.
- Mobile phones, computer games and MP3 players are solitary occupations, often without the involvement of another person, and certainly without the added messages of eye contact, facial expression and body language. Practitioners should bear in mind that the parent who spends much of their time texting or listening to their iPod will not be communicating as much with their child.
- Background music from the radio or television disrupts attention and restricts hearing. Music is a useful tool for practitioners but it should not be used indiscriminately. Keep music at a suitable volume and for particular activities – don't use it as 'aural wallpaper'!